GREAT DAYS OF
THE CIRCUS

RINGLING BROS·
COMBINI

CONGRESS OF WORLD-FAMOUS HORSE ACTS I
HUNDREDS OF BEAUTIFUL MARVELOUSLY TRAINED H

BARNUM & BAILEY
SHOWS

DUCED BY ALL EUROPE'S GREATEST TRAINERS.

MORE THAN FIFTY PRESENTED IN A SINGLE NUMBER.

GREAT DAYS OF

SECOND EDITION

Library of Congress Catalog Card Number: 62-12907
© 1962 by American Heritage Publishing Co., Inc., 551 Fifth Avenue, New York, New York 10017. All rights reserved under Berne and Pan-American Copyright Conventions. Trademark AMERICAN HERITAGE JUNIOR LIBRARY registered United States Patent Office.

THE CIRCUS

BY THE EDITORS OF
AMERICAN HERITAGE
The Magazine of History

NARRATIVE BY
FREEMAN HUBBARD

IN CONSULTATION WITH
LEONARD V. FARLEY
Librarian, Harry Hertzberg Circus Collection,
San Antonio Public Library

PUBLISHED BY
AMERICAN HERITAGE PUBLISHING CO., INC.
New York

INSTITUTIONAL AND BOOK TRADE DISTRIBUTION BY
HARPER & ROW

5644

Foreword

This book tells the story of an amusement. It is an important amusement, for in its early days the circus gave young, awkward America a view of the glamorous outside world; indeed, it was almost the only entertainment our grandparents had to watch. In its later, greater days between the two World Wars the circus provided perhaps the most popular entertainment available to all the people.

This is a history of the stars, stalwart as any pioneers, who, day after day, in colorful, exotic costumes performed thrilling, unbelievable feats under a canvas Big Top set in whatever vacant field they could find. The circus was born in Europe, but it grew to manhood in this country; and so firm is its place in American life that many of its peculiar expressions have become part of American speech. From dog-eared scrapbooks and dusty albums, from America's leading circus collections and the memoirs of great showmen, the story has been assembled. Many of the finely lithographed prints and posters shown here have not been reproduced in color since they were plastered on the barns, store fronts, and fences of backwoods America many years ago.

The moving of the long columns of circus wagons, animals, and troupers reflects the progress in the transportation systems that tied the country together. Whatever means there were—mud track, river boat, or railroad—the circus used them, and what it used it touched with magic and changed. The mud-spattered column was transformed into the high-stepping, glittering circus parade; the wagons into gorgeously carved and gilded floats; the old side-wheelers into floating palaces; and the "steam cars," as Americans called early trains, eventually became the long, brightly painted, incredibly efficient circus trains.

The humbug, the trickery, and the perpetual promises of the circus helped to mold a sense of humor peculiarly American. We learned not to mind being fooled—in fact, we expected it as part of the circus. We learned to accept hoaxes in which the whole public played the part of the bumpkin. When P. T. Barnum said, "The public likes to be fooled," he revealed the secret of why we laugh at ourselves, and why the circus has a special place in our most treasured memories.

The circus still goes on. In the summertime all over the country it brings once again the danger, the laughter, and the unique kind of tinseled, ephemeral beauty it has brought since John Bill Ricketts performed in eighteenth-century Philadelphia and Yankee Robinson slogged over the muddy southern roads of the early nineteenth century. If its arrival on Circus Day no longer has quite the excitement of the old days, it is because its influence has taken root in other entertainment forms and in advertising. Now it must compete with them.

Stripped to its essentials, the circus—always ancient yet always new—is much the same as it always was. Once inside the tent or the arena, peanuts in hand and mouth agape with amazement, the child of today gets the same visions as the child of long ago. Magic has come to him—just for a day.

LEONARD V. FARLEY

This 1899 Forepaugh & Sells poster records the spectacular fi-nale of an old-time circus. The drums roll, the clowns cavort, and the whole company of acrobats somersaults over massed elephants.

A number of AMERICAN HERITAGE
JUNIOR LIBRARY *books are published each year.*
Titles currently available are:

GEORGE WASHINGTON AND THE MAKING OF A NATION
CAPTAINS OF INDUSTRY
CARRIER WAR IN THE PACIFIC
JAMESTOWN: FIRST ENGLISH COLONY
AMERICANS IN SPACE
ABRAHAM LINCOLN IN PEACE AND WAR
AIR WAR AGAINST HITLER'S GERMANY
IRONCLADS OF THE CIVIL WAR
THE ERIE CANAL
THE MANY WORLDS OF BENJAMIN FRANKLIN
COMMODORE PERRY IN JAPAN
THE BATTLE OF GETTYSBURG
ANDREW JACKSON, SOLDIER AND STATESMAN
ADVENTURES IN THE WILDERNESS
LEXINGTON, CONCORD AND BUNKER HILL
CLIPPER SHIPS AND CAPTAINS
D-DAY, THE INVASION OF EUROPE
WESTWARD ON THE OREGON TRAIL
THE FRENCH AND INDIAN WARS
GREAT DAYS OF THE CIRCUS
STEAMBOATS ON THE MISSISSIPPI
COWBOYS AND CATTLE COUNTRY
TEXAS AND THE WAR WITH MEXICO
THE PILGRIMS AND PLYMOUTH COLONY
THE CALIFORNIA GOLD RUSH
PIRATES OF THE SPANISH MAIN
TRAPPERS AND MOUNTAIN MEN
MEN OF SCIENCE AND INVENTION
NAVAL BATTLES AND HEROES
THOMAS JEFFERSON AND HIS WORLD
DISCOVERERS OF THE NEW WORLD
RAILROADS IN THE DAYS OF STEAM
INDIANS OF THE PLAINS
THE STORY OF YANKEE WHALING

American Heritage also publishes
HORIZON CARAVEL BOOKS, *a similar series*
on world history, culture, and the arts.
Titles currently available are:

THE SPANISH ARMADA
BUILDING THE SUEZ CANAL
MOUNTAIN CONQUEST
PHARAOHS OF EGYPT
LEONARDO DA VINCI
THE FRENCH REVOLUTION
CORTES AND THE AZTEC CONQUEST
CAESAR
THE UNIVERSE OF GALILEO AND NEWTON
THE VIKINGS
MARCO POLO'S ADVENTURES IN CHINA
SHAKESPEARE'S ENGLAND
CAPTAIN COOK AND THE SOUTH PACIFIC
THE SEARCH FOR EARLY MAN
JOAN OF ARC
EXPLORATION OF AFRICA
NELSON AND THE AGE OF FIGHTING SAIL
ALEXANDER THE GREAT
RUSSIA UNDER THE CZARS
HEROES OF POLAR EXPLORATION
KNIGHTS OF THE CRUSADES

Contents

ILLUSTRATED WITH PAINTINGS, PRINTS, DRAW-
INGS, POSTERS, AND PHOTOGRAPHS OF THE PERIOD

CULVER PICTURES

1.
Circus Day

Circus Day in America once seemed as much a holiday as the Fourth of July.

Weeks ahead of time, a feeling of excitement began to creep over the town. First, over the rain-stained election posters and the faded auction signs there appeared suddenly, as if they had bloomed overnight, the huge, bright circus posters. Inhaling the pungent smell of poster paste, boys and girls stood before them and gawked.

No color was too bright, no word too big for the circus: THE MOST STUPENDOUS . . . WORLD FAMOUS . . . GREATEST . . . BRAVEST . . . WILDEST. . . . The posters promised lady acrobats in pink tights and elephants from the exotic East, snarling lions from darkest Africa and aerialists daring beyond belief.

The Circus is Coming, *painted in 1871 by Charles Caleb Ward, records the arrival of gaudy circus posters in a small Midwest town.*

Along with the eagerness, however, came worries: Would school be let out? Would it rain? Would parents supply the price of admission? Time seemed to stand still, for like the Fourth of July or Halloween, Circus Day drew nearer with agonizing slowness.

The circus always rented the vacant lot closest to town. The rest of the year it was just another weedy field; Circus Day made it seem the most important piece of real estate in the county.

The children of the town, especially the boys, knew all the trains—they knew what time it was by the whistle of number six or number thirteen, or by the heavy, long rumble of the through freights. That one train, the circus train, everybody knew. Farmers would look up from early morning chores and know it was rolling in. All the boys within running distance, and all the girls who were lucky enough to be taken to see it, were there to watch it come in.

The gleaming gold-and-red circus train that carried "the most colossal and stupendous show of all time!" was itself on the colossal and stupendous side. There were scores of cars—most of them oversize. Instead of the usual forty to fifty feet, circus cars were sometimes as long as seventy feet.

As the wheels stopped rolling, the traditional cry of "All out" released a horde of razorbacks—train loaders who pushed gaudy wagons with sunburst wheels down the loading platforms from the long flatcars. Whistles blew, bosses shouted, horses stamped—skittish from their overnight ride—and behind all the clatter was the distant roar and moan of hungry jungle beasts.

Then out of the tall stock-car doorways trundled the ponderous elephants, delicate on great tree-trunk feet. Each one came out and down the ramp in answer to its name. With trunks as clever as fingers they would find dirt and grass and toss it onto their backs to protect their thick wrinkled hides from insects. Even the baby elephants looked old and wise and tired.

Long before the performing artists left the train, the children of the town trooped to the circus ground behind the huge rolled tent (the Big Top), the tent poles, and the stacks of knockdown seats. Here the boys could earn free passes for watering the elephants—carrying bucket after bucket until their arms ached with pleasure and importance.

A full acre of canvas lay ready in

As the circus train arrives at dawn, townspeople gather to see the elephants unloaded (above left) and put to work raising the Big Top (above). Below left, a guying-out gang drives tent stakes. Below, a boy earning his free pass learns the size of an elephant's thirst.

13

the field. The first pole up, the king pole, was hauled into place by elephants in harness, straining against heavy chains. Up went the center poles. Then the elephants hauled the bale rings into place at the tops of the center poles, and the tent slowly billowed out, while the roustabouts chanted, "Heave it, weave it, shake it, break it, move along." The side walls flapped like sails. The guying-out gang sang, "Ah, hebie, hebby, hobby, hole . . ." in precise rhythm as they drove stakes for the guy ropes with sixteen-pound sledge hammers.

It took from two to four hours to raise the Big Top, and the empty field was fast transformed into a canvas city. The menagerie tent went up, then the side show with its line of gaudily painted banners: exciting jungle scenes, black-and-yellow-painted snakes curled around the bodies of pretty girls, shaggy-haired wild men from Borneo, a woman being sawed in half.

Refreshment trailers and ticket wagons were wheeled into place along the midway leading to the main entrance. To the smells of hay, sawdust, and animals were soon added the aromas of hot dogs and candied popcorn. The machine that spun out pink, fluffy candy was already turning. Men with great clusters of bright balloons and whirligig birds on strings touted them to the crowd watching the tent go up. There was a brisk sale of chameleons, those magical little creatures that change color rapidly, each one wear-

THREE STUPENDOUSLY MAG
TWELVE [

THE STROBRIDGE LITH CO
NY LONDON

MELODIOUS PARADE FEATURES INCLUDED IN
ERENT KINDS OF MUSIC.

Barnum & Bailey's parade featured these music wagons. The bell wagon in the background imitated the famous chimes of Bow Church in London. The steam calliope (center) could be heard for five miles, and the orchestmelochor (foreground) was an equally noisy organ.

ing a tiny gold collar and chain.

Soon the spectators headed back to Main Street. The Grand Cortege was forming on the circus lot, and there was a scramble for good places to see it pass. Excitement rippled like wildfire through the crowd waiting along the route. The more agile scuttled through the audience and stood at the very edge of the sidewalk, peering down the empty, familiar street. Away in the distance came the faint clop-clop of horses, hollow on pavement. Suddenly somebody down the street yelled, "Here it comes!" There was a tantivy of trumpets, and the band in the distance struck up the tune that sent shivers up every spine—"The Entry of the Gladiators."

The street was alive with noise as the first four lovely ladies on horseback, trumpets lifted to their lips, came into sight. They were always lithe and lovely, and the plumes they wore danced as their horses pranced. Then came the band, in red uniforms with gold braid, riding on a gilded band wagon that was sometimes drawn by as many as forty horses. The band never stopped playing: the big bass drum thumped steadily, the trumpets shrilled and blared, the cymbals flashed in the sun. Behind the band came great floats out of storybooks—Cinderella, Sleeping Beauty, Cossacks, Indians—and more equestrian ladies, riding sidesaddle.

The long line of elephants swayed along slowly, holding on to each other "trunk to tail" and driven by turbaned mahouts, or elephant trainers. Arrogant-looking camels lurched past. Cages of wild animals rumbled by, within them lions and tigers pacing nervously, roaring and grumbling.

"Hold your horses, here come the elephants!" was the warning cry as the parade began, for the scent of the strange beasts made horses shy. The 1911 photograph at left shows the Ringling circus parading in Lewiston, Maine.

Below is a part of the Campbell brothers' circus in 1908, lined up and waiting for the parade to begin. These are animal wagons. A lion paces nervously in the cage at the far right as a Mexican band on the roof tunes up.

Then the snake wagon rolled by. No one could see into it, but on its sides were painted great reptiles.

Around and through the procession roamed the clowns, riding donkeys or old Ford cars or little wagons drawn by goats. The music never stopped; there were many bands in many colors, and as one passed out of sight the next took over with a different march until the brass sounds crossed in the ears. All too soon—for many people could not go to the circus, and the parade was their free show—came the big tuneful steam calliope, signaling the end of the parade.

By afternoon, the tent city was massed with people, and there was a steady roar of noise: barkers and pitchmen, somewhere a band playing, in

the distance the shrill scales of a brass horn. In front of the side show, on the "bally" platform, the barker was giving his spiel. Veiled cootch dancers beside him wiggled a little to get the crowds to come inside. They looked aloof and bored, and it was disappointing to see one of the ladies "especially brought from a sultan's harem at great cost and danger" chewing gum. But nothing

rankled for long; there was too much else to see.

Inside the Big Top, the enormous tent was coming alive. Crowds shuffled in along the hippodrome, the outside track around the three rings, and clattered up the high tiers of blue seats. There was the smell of sawdust as a man raked it in the center ring; at the top of the tent could be seen a

In the 1880's when circus owner Adam Forepaugh found children seeking a free worm's-eye view of his show (like the boys above), he often let them in after the performance had started.

At left, a side show barker, aided by brightly painted banners and a row of Indians and cootch dancers, attracts a crowd. Most of the side show freaks were people with pathetic deformities.

19

The show began with the circus company circling the hippodrome in the Grand Entry. This 1890 lithograph includes Roman soldiers, lady charioteers, bareback riders, camels, elephants, and caged lions.

great web of aerial rigging, trapezes, and polished rings. Clowns mingled with the audience, flirting with the ladies and doing tricks for the children.

Into the center ring walked an erect, elegant man in a red coat, top hat, and polished black boots. Here was the ringmaster on whom the whole timing of the circus performance depended—and when that performance began, it went at a pace ("no waits, no breaks") that would make the next two hours seem like fifteen minutes.

The ringmaster's voice boomed into every corner of the Big Top—"La-adies and Gentlemen. . . !" First was the Grand Entry. Around the hippodrome came all the performers of the circus —charioteers, mounted cowboys, aerialists in spangled tights and long cloaks, lady bareback riders in short tutus, liberty horses (those that performed alone) with their tossing plumes, trained zebras, and funny floats covered with clowns, most of whom fell off at one point or another. The whole procession swept past to the wild circus march.

At a single blast from the ringmaster's whistle the air was suddenly alive with aerialists as the flying squadron shinnied up the ropes. With their gauze capes they seemed to fly like birds to the top of the tent. Everything happened, or seemed to happen, at once. In the end rings patient horses circled at a canter while a girl who looked like a child danced along their backs; in the center ring was a trapeze act. At a whistle it all appeared to change without stopping. While the cage for a wild animal act was being erected, the band played throbbing, junglelike music; and down front a clown labored over a huge sausage machine, while another fell over his yard-long, flapping feet.

The afternoon swept on, and such wonders as Royal Bengal tigers, fierce Numidian lions, a horn-playing seal, and dancing elephants thrilled the audience. The music never stopped except at moments when silence was more eloquent than music, as when the man on the high wire was going to do a "death-defying" trick. During these dramatic, breath-taking moments the drums would roll to heighten the suspense.

The performance seemed to be over almost as soon as it began. Children wandered out with the shuffling crowd, tired yet hardly believing it was over, wishing they might be brought back for the evening performance.

Late in the night there came that extra-lonesome, echoing train whistle that meant the circus was gone for another year. Tomorrow the field would be empty again except for a few spangles and popcorn cartons. Soon the gaudy posters on walls and fences would fade and flap in the wind, the last, lingering reminders of Circus Day.

Circus Day was over. The Greatest Show on Earth had packed up and moved on, and drab notices would soon cover the gay posters.

SCREEN STAR
BARNETT
3 RING CIRCUS
COUNTY
AIR
13-17 '38
AND NIGHTS
MIDWAY
PARIS, ME.

2.
Trick
Riders
and
Mud
Shows

This colorful eighteenth-century print shows a French troupe performing outdoors. The acrobatics, tumbling, and wire walking had changed very little since ancient times.

The circus is a very old form of entertainment that originated in ancient Rome. The very word "circus," in fact, comes from the Latin word for circle. In the Roman circus exotic animals and acrobats, and even real sea battles, were shown within a circle around which people sat.

The Roman circus was huge; it lasted all day, and parts of it were very cruel. Still, much of it is recognizable today. Pictures exist on the walls of a former Roman stable which show a ropedancer dancing with big, sacklike boots on an almost invisible rope. Even then, jugglers cavorted wildly, and entertainers leaped through fiery hoops. Androcles, the slave who took a thorn from the lion's paw and then was saved by the lion in the arena, was a favorite at the Roman circus. He might be called the first lion tamer.

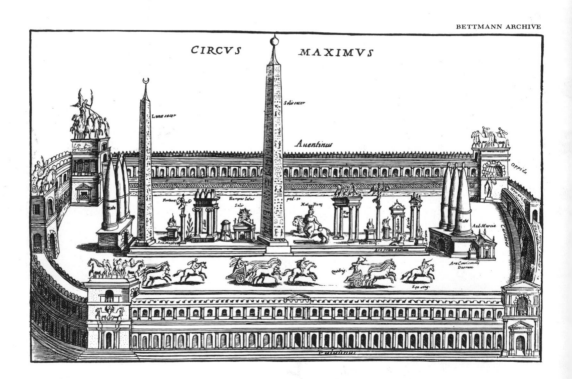

As many as 400,000 people could sit in the Circus Maximus of ancient Rome. A chariot race, perhaps its most famous event, is shown in the old engraving above. Drivers raced seven laps around the hippodrome.

At the age of seven Andrew Ducrow joined the first modern circus, that of Philip Astley in London, and grew to be Astley's top rider. In this 1817 lithograph (right) he performs in the costume of a Roman gladiator.

26

(Androcles and his lion wandered around the taverns of Rome, and people would give them both wine.) Chariot races, which were held in the Circus Maximus, were the most popular sport in Rome; the track around the modern circus is still called the hippodrome after the Latin word meaning horse course.

All throughout Europe for centuries jugglers, acrobats, magicians, and zan-ies (clowns) roamed from town to town and castle to castle, performing at fairs and on feast days, but not until 1770 in England did the circus as we know it begin. It began, as circuses should, with horses—horses on a circular track—and a young English cavalry sergeant named Philip Astley.

Astley was already a hero at the age of nineteen for charging and breaking the French line during the Seven Years'

War. For this feat he was made a sergeant major. He was tall, handsome, and a daring rider. One day in 1770 the city of London was littered with handbills announcing "Activity on Horseback by Mr. Astley, Sergeant-Major in His Majesty's Light Dragoons."

His trick riding performance included galloping full tilt around the ring, with one foot on the saddle and the other on the horse's head while he brandished a broadsword, and then riding balanced upside down atop the saddle. Gradually he added to his show: a human pyramid of acrobats, dancing dogs, wire walkers, a clown, and even a freak of sorts—a demure French lady whose golden hair was so long it trailed to the ground.

So the modern circus was born. The standard Astley used for the size of the circus ring, forty-two feet in diameter,

Wandering eighteenth-century showmen, like this one, often sold ribbons, buttons, or patent medicines in American frontier settlements while they showed their trained animals.

is still followed by many outfits all over the world. In 1782 one of his best riders, Charles Hughes, set up a rival show in London. Among Hughes's employees was a young man named John Bill Ricketts, who decided it was time the circus came to the New World.

In America in the late eighteenth century a few entertainers roamed the countryside with high-wire acts or trained animals, just as they had for centuries in Europe. The first lion to reach this country came in 1770, and a year later Americans saw a camel, but it took a master showman like Ricketts to present a real circus.

In a new country where cities and towns were isolated by distance and by almost impassable mud roads, people depended on horses not only for entertainment and pleasure but also for transportation. They admired fine horses and fine riders, so when Ricketts set up what he advertised as an English-type riding school in Philadelphia, horse lovers flocked to see him. It was no wonder that George Washington was at Ricketts' grand opening in what was then the nation's capital, on April 3, 1793.

Raised on a Virginia plantation, the President was an expert horseman himself. He watched Ricketts, astride his trick horse Cornplanter, jump over obstacles massed side by side, circle the ring with a boy standing on his shoulders, leap through a hoop twelve feet above the ground, do a juggling act, and dance in the saddle as his mount galloped around the ring.

THE
ELEPHANT,

ACCORDING to the account of the celebrated BUFFON, is the moſt reſpectable Animal in the world. In ſize he ſurpaſſes all other terreſtrial creatures; and by his intelligence, makes as near an approach to man, as matter can approach ſpirit. A ſufficient proof that there is not too much ſaid of the knowledge of this animal is, that the Proprietor having been abſent for ten weeks, the moment he arrived at the door of his apartment, and ſpoke to the keeper, the animal's knowledge was beyond any doubt confirmed by the cries he uttered forth, till his Friend came within reach of his trunk, with which he careſſed him, to the aſtoniſhment of all thoſe who ſaw him. This moſt curious and ſurpriſing animal is juſt arrived in this town, from Philadelphia, where he will ſtay but a few days.————He is only four years old, and weighs about 3000 weight, but will not have come to his full growth till he ſhall be between 30 and 40 years old. He meaſures from the end of his trunk to the tip of his tail 15 feet 8 inches, round the body 10 feet 6 inches, round his head 7 feet 2 inches, round his leg above the knee 3 feet 3 inches, round his ankle 2 feet 2 inches. He eats 130 weight a day, and drinks all kinds of ſpirituous liquors; ſome days he has drank 30 bottles of porter, drawing the corks with his trunk. He is ſo tame that he travels looſe, and has never attempted to hurt any one. He appeared on the ſtage, at the New Theatre in Philadelphia, to the great ſatisfaction of a reſpectable audience.

A reſpectable and convenient place is fitted up adjoining the Store of Mr. Bartlet, Market-Street, for the reception of thoſe ladies and gentlemen who may be pleaſed to view the greateſt natural curioſity ever preſented to the curious, which is to be ſeen from ſunriſe till ſundown, every day in the week.

☞ The Elephant having deſtroyed many papers of conſequence, it is recommended to viſitors not to come near him with ſuch papers.

Admittance *ONE QUARTER OF A DOLLAR*————Children *ONE EIGHTH OF A DOLLAR.*

NEWBURYPORT, Sept. 19, 1797.

The first elephant arrived in America in 1796 and toured the East for over twenty years. This handbill claims that he once drank thirty bottles of ale, "drawing the corks with his trunk."

An unknown nineteenth-century artist painted this charming view of George Washington on his prancing white charger Jack. John Bill Ricketts exhibited Jack in the first American circus.

Washington had a white charger named Jack that he had ridden as commander in chief in the Revolutionary War. When Jack was twenty-eight years old and had long since been put out to pasture, Ricketts made an offer to pay $150 to the President to display Jack in a stall at the circus. Washington accepted. Thus the Father of his Country made a deal with the Father of the American Circus, and the new venture got its first side show.

Ricketts' circus did so well that he built a new home for it in Philadelphia, a white amphitheatre with tall, slender columns in front. On top of the conical roof he put a weathervane shaped like the Roman god Mercury, the messenger. In the autumn of 1794 Ricketts took his show on a wagon tour, traveling as far north as New York and Boston and as far south as Baltimore. In 1797, when the President retired to private life, Ricketts put on a special program for him.

On December 17, 1799, three days after Washington died, disaster struck the nation's first circus. Fire destroyed the Philadelphia amphitheatre. Ricketts gave up in despair and sailed for England; on the voyage the ship was lost with everyone aboard.

Other circuses soon sprang up along the Atlantic coast. So many originated in the small area including Somers and Brewster, New York, and part of nearby Connecticut that it is known as the Cradle of the American Circus. From there "mud shows" (so called because of the muddy roads they had to travel

We ne'er shall look upon his like again

The celebrated Cornplanter *taking a flying leap over* Silva *a Horse of his own height*

Ricketts' equestrian ability made him the star of his own circus and a favorite of President Washington. Above, he takes a "flying leap" on his trick horse Cornplanter.

Overleaf: This handsome and rare Spalding & Rogers poster advertises an equestrian show by the Humpty Dumpty Pantomime Troupe in New York about 1855.

on) spread over the whole country. By 1820 at least thirty wagon shows were touring the United States. They played in barns, theatres, or outdoors before nothing more than a canvas backdrop nailed to a building.

One notable event took place in 1815 when Hachaliah Bailey, a young showman from Somers, went down to New York to meet his brother, a sea captain. The captain had bought an elephant for twenty dollars in London and sold the animal to his brother for $1,000, making a tidy profit of 5,000 per cent on his investment. Hachaliah named his elephant Old Bet and began to tour the country with her. He displayed her mostly in barns, traveling over the rutted, lonely country roads at night to keep curious folks from seeing her free of charge. His partner, Nathan Howes, was not so careful. One hot July afternoon Howes was leading the huge, patient beast along a road in Maine, when a farmer, hiding behind a tree, shot her.

The farmer's motive is not recorded. Perhaps he was testing the boast that Old Bet's hide was bulletproof, perhaps she had scared his horses (or him), or perhaps he was one of the fanatical puritans of the period who thought all entertainment sinful. Hachaliah sadly buried his pet beside the Elephant Hotel which he had built at Somers and marked the spot with a tall granite pillar crowned by a gold-lacquered wooden statue of her. The hotel is now a pioneer circus museum, and the stone monument is still stand-

ing. One hundred years later, in 1927, one of the Ringling Bros. and Barnum & Bailey elephants was walked fifty-six miles from New York City to Somers to lay a wreath on Old Bet's grave.

After the death of Old Bet, Nathan Howes joined Aaron Turner, a Ridgebury, Connecticut, shoemaker, to organize a wagon show. They made history by pitching a round tent, ninety feet in diameter, for their shows—the earliest Big Top. On a breezy day it sounded like a windjammer under full sail. The Turner Circus, as it was known, rode in four heavily carved, gilded wagons, each pulled by two work horses, with a fine, showy ring steed cavorting in the rear.

They rolled through the East and the South into towns so isolated that the visit of a fiddle-playing peddler would be discussed for a week. In these sections of the country almost the only entertainments were public hangings, militia musters, election days, and religious tent meetings. Few people grew up without going to the revival meetings which were usually held in wooded areas on the edges of the towns. They traveled by foot, on horseback, in buggies or in wagons to listen to a full week of hell-fire-and-damnation preaching by sometimes as many as fifty circuit-riding preachers. It was almost their only relief from drab frontier loneliness.

Then came the Turner Circus. The shrill, fast, brassy march from the band cut through the silent boredom of the dirt main street; the ponderous red-

This 1847 traveling menagerie featured a Chrysarma—simply a fancy name for a parade wagon.

and-gold circus wagons rumbled past the unpainted store fronts; the one trick horse pranced and reared. If the shutters were closed against the sinful circus in the more respectable houses, the whole rest of the town and county around—black and white, old and young—ran, tumbled, and shoved to gawk at the glamour, the silver stars, the spangles, the gaiety, and the raucous noise of the circus. School was not dismissed; the children simply ran when they heard the drums. No matter how much warning there was from the clergy and the newspaper of "traveling death" and "moral ruin," nobody worked on Circus Day. Boys dreamed of running away to follow the circus, and so many did that it gave showmen the reputation of being child stealers. The circus was wild and it was foreign —even its bright colors were "sinful."

America was still strongly puritanical. As far west as Cincinnati, men were fined or jailed for riding a horse on Sunday or playing cards or billiards

any day. Although Congress had long since repealed a Revolutionary War law against theatrical shows, and although Washington and other Presidents had been seen at circuses, it was a common occurrence for the press and the clergy to denounce them. A Staten Island newspaper complained that a single visit of the Great Eastern circus took from the community "enough money to sustain three missionaries among the heathen for a year."

Managers did what they could to combat religious prejudice against their shows. Isaac Van Amburgh, the first wild-animal trainer in America, quoted the Bible to justify his touring menagerie. He argued that since God had created man and made him superior to the beasts of the field, it was a religious act for trained animals to kneel at his feet!

The rural camp meeting, a week-long blend of religion and outdoor picnicking, was one of the few entertainments, besides the circus, that was available to the American frontier.

Not only the clergy gave the circus men trouble. They had to be as tough as the hickory clubs they often used to defend themselves. Most frontier towns were gathering places for backwoods rowdies, and pitched battles between the circus people and the local bullies were so common that for years showmen carried guns. When a showman was attacked, his rallying cry, "Hey Rube!" brought immediate help from his comrades and usually started a general brawl, or "clem."

There was some reason for local prejudice. Circuses tended to be more poetic than truthful in their advertising, and local people hated to be tricked. Also, card sharps and pickpockets followed the circus caravans and mixed with the crowds.

But with all the hardships faced by the early mud shows, the industry grew. A group of very respectable businessmen around Brewster sent out show after show. Even faraway California soon had its own circus. Joseph A. Rowe was only ten when he ran away from his North Carolina home to join the circus. In 1849 he launched his own show at San Francisco in a tent jammed with 1,500 gold rush prospectors. Rowe and his wife played the gold mining camps in the hills, accepting gold dust for admission tickets. Then they toured the South Sea islands and entertained Kamehameha, the native king of Hawaii, and his wives and subjects. On another tropical island, according to Rowe's memoirs, a curious man-eating tribe en-

joyed his program. "Seemingly the cannibals were also beguiled of their appetites," he wrote, "as the company, after showing for a while, embarked on their vessel and no one was reported missing."

With land transport so difficult, many circuses took to the water. As early as 1815 a circus boat floated down the Ohio River, and ten years later the Erie Canal had a showboat which went to the Great Lakes. In 1852 the most magnificent of showboats was built by Gilbert Spalding and Charles J. Rogers. They called it the *Floating Palace*. It had two side-wheel towboats, the *Banjo* and the *James Raymond*. Inside the two-story wooden structure were a regulation circus ring, a stage, and a large auditorium. It was lit by gas and heated by steam pipes. As many as 2,500 people could watch the circus— some of them paying a dollar just to stand on the deck and look through the windows. Chimes erected on the roof of the *Floating Palace* would herald its approach; later, a steam calliope replaced the bells.

Many great showmen came out of the Cradle of the American Circus, but one man was their prince—the Prince of Humbugs—who revolutionized American entertainment. P. T. Barnum changed American taste, and he made the country laugh.

Isaac Van Amburgh, not content with being America's leading trainer, called himself "the greatest lion tamer in the world." In 1839 he reached the peak of fame with a command performance before England's Queen Victoria.

M^R VAN AMBURGH

The Grand Spectacle of **CHARLEMAGNE** *nightly represented*

at the **THEATRE ROYAL DRURY LANE.**

INTERIOR VIEW OF SPALDING & ROGERS FLOATING PALACE.

FLOATING PALACE.

The Floating Palace *carried the Spalding & Rogers circus to the towns along the Mississippi and Ohio rivers in the 1850's. This glamorous showboat, which cost $42,000 to build, was lit by 200 gas jets and decorated with red velvet draperies and ornate carvings. In the print at left equestrians perform in the single ring; the smaller pictures show other featured acts. Above, the* Floating Palace *and her towboat ride out a "memorable storm" off Mobile, Alabama, in 1853. She toured the rivers for ten years, sat out the Civil War tied to a wharf, and was destroyed by fire in 1865.*

3.

The Prince of Humbugs

Phineas Taylor Barnum was born July 5, 1810, in Bethel, Connecticut. After a start as bookkeeper, ticket seller, and emergency tent pitcher for forty dollars a month in the first traveling tent circus in America, he became a millionaire showman and built for himself what President Ulysses S. Grant once said was the best-known name in all the world. He hoaxed, bamboozled, tricked, shocked, and entertained the American public of the nineteenth century, and they loved him for it. There is no proof that he actually said, "There's a sucker born every minute," but whether he said it or not, it was the principle on which he built his fabulous career.

Sad-eyed Phineas Taylor Barnum, photographed here by Mathew Brady, was called by some a crook and a swindler, by others a genius and the "Shakespeare of Advertising."

Even as a boy, Phineas was shrewd. His father died when he was fifteen. The eldest of five children, he went to work in a general store where he managed to get rid of a wagonload of unsaleable green bottles for a high price in a legal gambling lottery scheme. Before he was eighteen he owned a fruit and confection store in Bethel and was selling lottery tickets on the side.

One of his customers was Hachaliah Bailey. Barnum idolized him; his tales about Old Bet set the boy in the small-town general store dreaming. But excited as he was by Hachaliah Bailey's stories, young Phineas Barnum was even fonder of another visitor to his store, the apple-cheeked Charity Hallett, and when he became nineteen he married her.

During the next few years Barnum held a long succession of jobs, and poverty was never very far away. In the days when all newspaper editors had to be armed to protect themselves from threatened shootings or horse-whippings by readers who happened to disagree with them, he published a small weekly newspaper in which he expressed himself so bluntly that he was sued for libel, paid a fine, and served sixty days in jail. On his release the twenty-two-year-old Barnum was hailed as a champion of the free press. Seated in a coach drawn by six horses, accompanied by the local band and preceded by forty horsemen, he rode home in triumph.

Phineas Barnum loved a parade. This brief hour of glory whetted his show-man's appetite—this and the knowledge that vast numbers of people had traveled for miles and paid a fortune to gawk at Old Bet. He began a long search for the exotic, tracking down every clue to what he wanted.

A friend mentioned having seen a dog with two tails, and Barnum wanted to buy it. It turned out to be a joke—an ordinary mutt had been seen carrying a calf's tail in its mouth. Barnum kept on searching for something to exhibit; fake or real, he didn't care, just

In his autobiography Barnum titled the fanciful drawing below My Delivery from Imprisonment. *The young editor was greeted by cheering crowds after a jail term for libel.*

Barnum had his first success with Joice Heth, whom his broadsides (right) claimed was 161 years old. Years after she was proved a fraud, he insisted he had believed the claims.

so long as it was strange or rare, exciting or new.

"The American people," Barnum said, "like to be humbugged." As a case in point, there was his Joice Heth hoax. In August, 1835, Barnum placed this advertisement in New York newspapers:

"The Greatest Natural & National Curiosity in the World. Joice Heth, nurse to General George Washington, (the Father of Our Country) . . . Joice Heth is unquestionably the most astonishing and interesting curiosity in the World! She was the slave of Augustine Washington, (the father of Gen. Washington,) and was the first person who put clothes on the unconscious infant who in after days led our heroic fathers on to glory, to victory, and to freedom. . . . Joice Heth was born . . . in the year 1674 and has consequently now arrived at the astonishing age of 161 years! She . . . sings numerous hymns, relates many interesting anecdotes of Gen. Washington. . . . She . . . takes great pleasure in conversing with Ministers and religious persons. . . . Original, authentic and indisputable documents prove that . . . Joice Heth is in every respect the person she is represented."

The documents, allegedly bills of sale for the colored slave signed by Augustine Washington, were later branded as frauds. But at first the people were too thrilled to be skeptical. Washington had died thirty-six years before and was already the new country's greatest hero. Crowds flocked to see the frail, blind, badly-crippled Negro woman. Barnum had learned about her from a guest at the boardinghouse that he and Charity were running in New York and had raised $1,000 to buy her. Afterwards he wrote in his life story, "I had at last found my true

GREAT ATTRACTION
At the Masonic Hall!

UNPARALLELED LONGEVITY.
FOR TWO DAYS ONLY.

JOICE HETH,
NURSE TO
Gen. George Washington,

(The father of our country) who has arrived at the astonishing age of **161** years! will be seen in the large room at the Masonic Hall, opposite the Franklin House, for TWO DAYS ONLY, as she is on her way to Boston, where she must be early next week.

JOICE HETH is unquestionably the most astonishing and interesting curiosity in the World! She was the slave of Augustine Washington, (the father of Gen. Washington,) and was the first person who put clothes on the unconscious infant who in after days led our heroic fathers on to glory, to victory, and to freedom. To use her own language when speaking of the illustrious Father of his country, "she raised him." JOICE HETH was born in the Island of Madagascar, on the Coast of Africa, in the year 1674 and has consequently now arrived at the astonishing

Age of 161 Years !

She weighs but forty-six pounds, and yet is very cheerful and interesting. She retains her faculties in an unparrelleled degree, converses freely, sings numerous hymns, relates many interesting anecdotes of Gen. Washington, the red coats, &c. and often laughs heartily at her own remarks, or those of the spectators. Her health is perfectly good, and her appearance very neat. She was baptized in the Potomac river and received into the Baptist Church 16 years ago, and takes great pleasure in conversing with Ministers and religious persons. The appearance of this marvellous relic of antiquity strikes the beholder with amazement, and convinces him that his eyes are resting on the oldest specimen of mortality they ever before beheld. Original, authentic and indisputable documents prove that however astonishing the fact may appear, JOICE HETH is in every respect the person she is represented.

The most eminent physicians and intelligent men both in New York and Philadelphia, have examined this *living skeleton* and the documents accompanying her, and all *invariably* pronounce her to be as represented 161 *years of age!* Indeed it's impossible for any person, however incredulous, to visit her without astonishment and the most perfect satisfaction that she is as old as represented.

A female is in continual attendance, and will give every attention to the ladies who visit this relic of by gone ages.

She was visited at Niblo's Garden, New York, by *ten thousand persons* in two weeks.———Hours of exhibition from 9 A. M. to 1 P. M. and from 4 to 10 P. M.—Admittance 25 cents—Children 12½ cents.

Overleaf: This exciting lithograph shows Jenny Lind, "The Swedish Nightingale," sleighing past the American Museum in New York. In 1850 Barnum brought the soprano to America, where she was a smash hit and had clothes, furniture, and a clipper ship named after her.
RINGLING MUSEUM OF THE CIRCUS

This cartoon, entitled Selling the Public, *accuses Barnum of using raucous publicity to promote Jenny Lind, just as if she were one of his freaks. He had New York at a fever pitch for her opening concert on September 11, 1850. Tickets sold for as much as $225. Castle Garden was packed with men—Barnum had advertised the small, plain singer as a great beauty—and the clamoring crowd outside nearly drowned out her voice. Her two-year tour made Jenny Lind a rich woman, and Barnum made a tidy profit of a quarter of a million dollars for himself.*

vocation." For about six months Barnum exhibited pathetic old Joice Heth in New York City and in New England. When she died in February, 1836, a famous surgeon made an autopsy of her shriveled body and reported that "instead of being 161 years old, she was probably not over eighty."

After giving a good funeral to his first property, Barnum took to the road with Aaron Turner's circus for a six-month tour, his first venture into the excitement and peril of the traveling circus business. Twenty-six years old, tall, sturdy, and good-humored, with curly hair and twinkling blue eyes, P. T. Barnum set out to discover nineteenth-century America.

As combined ticket seller and bookkeeper he received forty dollars a month plus one-fifth of the profits. He took with him Vivalla, a juggler he had under contract. When the Negro singer ran away from slavery, the undaunted Barnum blacked his face and sang the songs himself. When the little mud show reached North Carolina, Barnum decided to raise a small variety troupe of his own. Soon it was moving through the South known as Barnum's Grand Scientific and Musical Theatre. After a few months, Barnum and a partner bought an old side-wheeler for a new troupe, hired a crew, and steamed down the Mississippi to New Orleans, stopping at major boat landings to set up the tent and give performances. But this trip happened to coincide with the worst financial depression in the history of the young country. In 1838 Barnum's show flopped; empty-handed, he headed north to rejoin his family.

By now he had learned what the public wanted and what it would take. He knew how to advertise with pamphlets, posters, lectures, and by plant-

VANTILE MACK, THE INFANT LAMBERT, OR

GIANT BABY!!

7 Years old. Weighs 257 pounds!

Measures 61 inches around the chest.! 36 inches around the leg !!

With his Mother, only 24 years of age..

NOW EXHIBITING AT BARNUM'S AMERICAN MUSEUM.

ing controversial items in the newspapers. "Without printer's ink," he wrote, "I would have been no bigger than Tom Thumb."

Tom Thumb, his first great attraction, was born Charles Stratton, the son of a Connecticut carpenter. When Barnum first saw him, in 1842, Tom was almost five years old, weighed about fifteen pounds, and stood less than two feet tall. Barnum made a deal with his parents and promptly billed him as "General Tom Thumb, a dwarf of eleven years, just arrived from England." Truth was never a strong point in Barnum's advertising. (He also misused the word dwarf—a dwarf is a misshapen small person; Tom Thumb was a perfectly formed midget.)

Barnum exhibited him in his newly erected American Museum, a five-story building in New York which he filled with musty curiosities, freaks, wild animals, new inventions, and panoramas of Biblical scenes — all which he bought on credit. In tune with the respectable spirit of the time, he publicized the religious, moral, and educational values of his attractions. The main exhibition room of the sensational collection of freaks and fakes was always known as the Lecture Hall.

For years the American Museum was New York's most popular amusement. Its doors were opened at sunrise and stayed open until late at night. People brought baskets of lunch and spent the whole day being mystified. One hideous specimen was advertised as the Feejee Mermaid. It was made of

Typical of the attractions at Barnum's American Museum was the 257-pound "giant baby" shown at left with his mother. Barnum had huge posters made of the curiosities he had collected. On the museum roof were powerful floodlights, the brightest lights in New York.

Even the "professor" who lectured on the Feejee Mermaid (right) balked when Barnum hung an eighteen-foot painting of it outside the Museum. After seeing that, he said, the public would never accept "our dried-up specimen eighteen inches long"—but it did.

The Barnum stable of freaks include
these attractions. The Wild Men
Borneo (above left), called Plutano an
Waino by Barnum, were actually plai
Hiram and Barney Davis, and they ha
never been within 10,000 miles of Bo
neo. The original Siamese twins, Chan
and Eng (above), disliked each othe
and after quarreling might not spea
for days. The twins married sisters an
would live for a while in Chang's hom
then in Eng's. The Lucasie famil
(left) were true Albinos, with whit
hair and pink eyes. They came fro
Madagascar and were of Negro bloo

52

a monkey's head joined to a fish's body. The lively scientific controversy that raged around it meant more publicity for Barnum.

Other Barnum hoaxes included "the horse with its head where its tail ought to be" (a normal horse with its tail in a feeding stall), and a boldly painted sign reading "This Way to the Egress" hung alongside the directions leading to the lioness and the tigress. Once a visitor had gone through the door to see the egress he found himself in the street and had to pay another admission fee to see the other exhibits. Barnum called his humbugs "advertising skyrockets sent up to attract people to the great and instructive collections" in his museum.

He tried to lease the American side of Niagara Falls so he could fence it in and charge admission to tourists. He made offers for Madame Tussaud's waxworks gallery of famous people in London, for a tree on which the poet Lord Byron had carved his name, for the birthplace of William Shakespeare at Stratford on Avon. In 1858 he offered $5,000 for the privilege of sending the first message over the newly laid Atlantic cable. He tried to buy the "woman's dress" that Confederate President Jefferson Davis was supposedly wearing when he was captured in 1865. (When Barnum found out that it was actually Mrs. Davis' raglan coat, he lost interest.) But none of these things were for sale, even to fast-talking P. T. Barnum.

Chang and Eng, from Siam, were popular exhibits at the American Museum. They had a five and a half inch band connecting their chests, but were able to stand and move sideways together and even swim together. Although Chang and Eng had different temperaments and disliked each other, surgeons refused to cut the band on the ground that such an operation would be fatal.

Both men were married, and between them they fathered twenty-one children. Their family life was unique: after living for three days in Chang's home they would go to Eng's, a mile away, for three days; then back to Chang's and so on. In 1874 Chang collapsed at the age of sixty-three. Both men died the same day. Today any twins joined together at birth are known as Siamese twins.

Tom Thumb and the huge elephant Jumbo were Barnum's greatest stars. In 1844 Barnum took Tom to London, where they met Queen Victoria three times (for years afterward circus acts were advertised as "playing before the crowned heads of Europe"). Tom was displayed in London's Egyptian Hall; in the same building the romantic painter Benjamin Haydon was showing one of his huge canvases. The public ignored him. Haydon's journal told how Londoners "rush by thousands to see Tom Thumb. They push, they fight, they scream, they cry help and murder! and oh! and ah! They see my bills, my boards, my caravans and don't read them . . . It is an iniquity, a rabies, a madness. . . ." In despair, poor Haydon

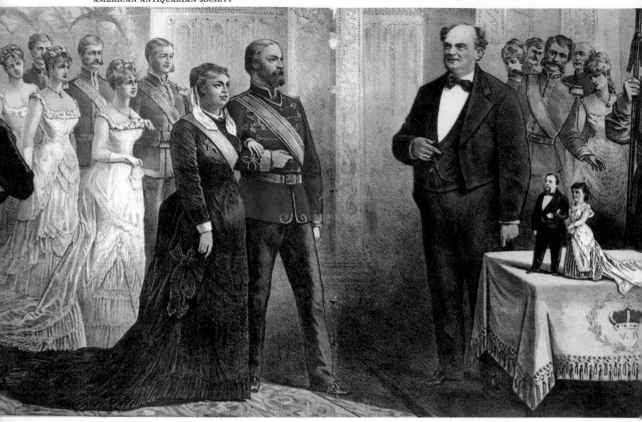

When Tom Thumb married a pretty midget schoolteacher named Lavinia Warren, two thousand guests came to their elegant wedding. This poster shows them with Barnum at the English court. While the Thumbs were indeed small, they were not as small as the artist has made them.

blew out his brains with a pistol, a scandal which made even more publicity for Barnum.

In 1851 the showman organized Barnum's Great Asiatic Caravan, Museum, and Menagerie, a circus which toured America for four years, and featured Tom Thumb riding a baby elephant. There were also 9 other elephants, 110 horses, 6 lions, a Burmese bull, and Mr. Nellis, the Armless Wonder. The American circus had grown with Barnum.

Tom Thumb married a midget named Lavinia. On their world-wide honeymoon the couple met Emperor Napoleon III of France, King Victor Emmanuel of Italy, and Pope Pius IX. In addition to what he earned for Barnum, Tom made several million dollars for himself, lived in luxury, and died in 1883 at the age of forty-five.

In the meantime Barnum was having troubles with the American Museum. On Thanksgiving night in 1864 Confederate spies set nineteen hotels ablaze in a Civil War plot to burn New York City. One of the saboteurs hurled a fire bomb at the Museum. Some 2,500 people fought their way out of the Lecture Hall through dense white smoke. The freaks and the wild animals were also brought out safely—all but Anna Swan, a giantess seven feet eleven inches tall, who panicked and had to be subdued by six firemen before she could be led from the building.

On July 13, 1865, fire broke out again at Barnum's museum, this time caused by a spark from the steam-powered air-cooling fans. A mob of thousands gathered on Broadway to watch Barnum's greatest show. A husky fireman staggered out half-carrying the 400-pound fat lady; when a Royal Bengal tiger leaped from a second-story window, a fireman killed it with an axe. Anna Swan, groping through the smoke to find her life's savings, $1,200, collapsed on the third floor.

"There was not a door through which her bulky frame could obtain passage," the New York *Tribune* reported. "It was likewise feared that the stairs would break down, even if she should reach them. Her best friend, the living skeleton, stood by her as long as he dared, but then deserted her." Finally, rescuers broke a window and used a derrick to haul the giantess to safety. While this was going on, firemen opened the cages of tropical birds on the top floor and let them fly over the city. The entire five-story structure and its collection were destroyed, except for a trained seal and several monkeys, snakes, and birds.

Barnum rallied his resources once more and built and stocked a new museum, but when on March 3, 1868, that too was destroyed by fire, the blow was too much. A few weeks later the Prince of Humbugs retired from show business at the age of fifty-eight. He did not know that events in the years ahead would make his name immortal in the American circus.

Barnum had his share of criticism, such as the caricature at left showing him as a "humbug."

Overleaf: In 1865, when the American Museum burned for the second time, Barnum's greatest crowd watched the holocaust. Snakes writhed up Broadway, and an ape walked into the newsroom of the New York Herald.
NEW-YORK HISTORICAL SOCIETY

The color and pageantry and the sheer size of the Grand Entry of a circus in the Golden Age were very nearly overwhelming. This is the Ringling Bros. and Barnum & Bailey show in 1934.

4.

The Golden Age

The word "family" is a familiar one in circus history—aerial families, animal-training families, clown families. But the circus' Golden Age made up the greatest family tree of all. Circus promoters intermarried, bought each other out, and merged through the years from the early 1870's until 1919, when the Greatest Show on Earth took its final, most memorable name—

Ringling Bros. and Barnum & Bailey.

The story of the Golden Age may be said to have begun one day in 1859 when Yankee Robinson's circus was seized by a mob of rabid southerners at Charleston, South Carolina, simply because they resented his name. He had to flee, leaving his property behind, and he never got it back. But soon he put together another show,

which was managed by William C. Coup, a former circus roustabout, and later Robinson hired an acrobat-juggler named Al Ringling. So three of the fathers of the Greatest Show on Earth were brought together.

A fourth famous circus name was born Jim McGinnis in Pontiac, Michigan. An orphan, McGinnis latched on to a circus promoter named Bailey, and in 1860 Bailey adopted the boy, giving him the name James Anthony Bailey. He began his career as a bill poster, and by 1881 he had risen so high in the canvas world that he challenged the mighty Barnum.

As the American West was developed, the circuses followed the settlers. Dan Costello, a veteran clown, organized a circus and menagerie, and was touring Dixie in 1869 when the driving of the golden spike in Utah completed the first transcontinental railroad. Costello immediately headed in that direction. En route they detrained, with two elephants, and marched eighty-five grueling miles over the mountains to Denver. The strain was too much for one of the elephants, a baby, which died in Colorado. "Mr. Costello," reported *The Rocky Mountain News,* "has taken a great risk in venturing so far from the railroad." Joyous crowds showed their appreciation by jamming the tent to capacity each performance.

In 1870 P. T. Barnum was sixty years old and living in retirement at Bridgeport, Connecticut, with little desire to return to show business. William Coup, who had advanced from

The dashing bareback rider, with his clown helper in this 1870 poster, was one of the star-ring acts of a nineteenth-century American circus. He has just jumped through the paper hoop held by the clown and landed with studied grace on the back of his handsome horse.

roustabout to ownership of his own circus, approached the Prince of Humbugs with the suggestion that with Costello they put together "a great traveling attraction." Barnum refused at first. "I have already done enough work," he told him, "and shall play the rest of my life."

But Coup persisted and won him over. Their new circus opened on April 10, 1871, at Brooklyn, New York, under nearly three acres of canvas—the largest Big Top people had ever seen. The exhibitions included such typical Barnum side show attractions as two mechanical breathing figures, the Sleeping Beauty and the Dying Zouave; live freaks such as the midget Admiral Dot, the Palestine Giant, and a family known as the Fiji Cannibals; and what was billed as the Cardiff Giant, a fraud monumental even for Barnum. The Giant, a huge body "discovered" buried on a farm in upper New York State, was a hoax. Unable to rent it, Barnum made his own Giant and insisted it was the original, thus promoting a hoax of a hoax.

Streaming banners proclaimed the P. T. Barnum Museum, Menagerie, and Circus, International Zoological Garden, Polytechnic Institute and Hippodrome. Coup was the manager; Barnum provided the foremost name in show business and a shrewd understanding of human nature; and Dan Costello supplied his skill and experience in getting up circus programs.

But it was really Coup, not Barnum, who created the show. Wherever he went, Coup induced the railroads to run half-rate Circus Day excursions. He used the newly developed lithograph steam press for mass production of huge posters in vivid colors. Spending money so wildly that he scared the aging Barnum, Coup plastered gaudy, evocative posters all over the towns within a fifty-mile radius of circus stands. Their train rolled by night so as not to cut into show time.

"I don't know much about running a circus," Barnum admitted, "but I know how to pick men who do."

One of the men he picked, however, was John V. O'Brien, better known as "Pogey." Pogey was a fat man who could neither read nor write more than a few words; he dressed like a "swell," wearing diamond-studded buttons on his double-breasted silk and velvet vest. Most showmen resented the extremes to which he carried the practices of shortchanging customers and allowing shady operators to use his midway. Most reputable circuses had long since "gone Sunday school," their term for cleaning up the midways.

Barnum lost considerable prestige when he split up his big show and leased part of it, plus the use of his name, to Pogey O'Brien. Rival showmen put out defamatory posters, called rat-sheets, that made much of the fact that Barnum's circus was divided. Bill Coup and Dan Costello were furious. They broke up the partnership and went into separate ventures of their own.

At about the same time, James A.

Bailey and James E. Cooper formed a combined circus and wild-animal show, with Bailey, the former orphan boy, as the top man. In 1876 they loaded their show into a sailing vessel and toured Tasmania, off the Australian coast. Their next stop was Sydney, Australia, but before they got there a hurricane sent mountainous waves tumbling over their ship. One by one the cages lashed to the deck were torn loose.

Bailey led the troupers and the ship's crew in a gallant effort to save the animals. Wild beasts screamed, bellowed, and snarled in the howling wind. The bewildered rhinoceros slipped into the sea with a mighty splash. Cage after cage followed until nearly half of the animals were gone. A giant wave knocked the spindly-legged giraffe off its feet and killed it.

When the battered ship docked at Sydney, Bailey had the giraffe's hide

Cooper & Bailey's circus lands in Australia in 1877 while on a world tour. Although a storm at sea killed their one giraffe, this poster shows two of them in fine health on the dock.

63

Ten Times the Largest and Best Show on Earth!

St. Joseph, WEDNESDAY, | SURE One Day ONLY! | JULY 23

COOPER, BAILEY & CO.'S
GREAT
International Allied Shows!

Having just Returned from a Grand Three Years Triumphal Tour Around the World,
Traveling 67,000 Miles by Land and Sea, have CONSOLIDATED FOR
THIS SEASON ONLY, with the

GREAT LONDON CIRCUS
And SANGER'S ROYAL BRITISH MENAGERIE.
FORMING A FORMIDABLE COMBINATION.

TWO SHOWS!   A DOUBLE CIRCUS!   TWO MENAGERIES!

IN OPERATION DAY & NIGHT At Every Performance

Resplendent Redolent Refulgent

FAINTLY DESCRIBES THE WONDERFUL

ELECTRIC LIGHT!

The Public Mind Dazed!   The Great Invention!
ALL OF OUR VAST PAVILIONS
LIGHTED BY ELECTRICITY.
168,000 YARDS OF CANVAS

Are used in the manufacture of the CIRCUS, MENA-
GERIE AQUARIUM and MUSEUM TENTS, all of
which are illuminated by the BRUSH ELECTRIC LIGHT, making night as bright as day. Giving a volume of light EQUAL
TO 35,000 GAS JETS. The entire population on the *qui vive* of expectation and curiosity to behold the real wonder of the
Nineteenth century. Already you hear the remark of thousands, "We are going to the Great London Show, to see

THE WONDERFUL ELECTRIC LIGHT.

The Mammoth Pavilion Illuminated at every Exhibition in the day time as well as night—The Electric Light in Constant
Operation. Every visitor to the Grand Exhibition exclaiming with wonder and delight

Beautiful! Marvelous! Grand!

stuffed by a taxidermist and equipped with a mechanism that nodded its head slowly. Shown in a darkened cage, it appeared to visitors as a living animal. Later, after buying more beasts, the show toured Australia and New Zealand. Bailey visited the Dutch East Indies and finally South Africa, returning to New York in 1879. He was now a seasoned veteran of thirty-one.

In 1880 the show became Cooper & Bailey's Great London Circus. That year, when they were playing Philadelphia, one of their elephants gave birth to Columbia, the first elephant born in America. This event was front-page news. Barnum noted the publicity with growing concern. He sent Bailey a telegram offering $100,000 for Columbia and her mother. Bailey not only refused, wiring Barnum to look to his laurels, but had a mammoth copy made of the telegram and featured it on posters under the title, "What Barnum Thinks of the Baby Elephant."

The old-timer met this challenge by merging with Bailey. After some financial juggling, the Barnum & London circus appeared, with Barnum, Bailey, and James Hutchinson as proprietors. Later on, Hutchinson sold his shares, and the names Barnum and Bailey appeared together in 1881 for the first time in the world of the circus.

The Golden Age reached its first

When electricity first lit the circus, it was hailed as an exotic new attraction in the 1879 poster at left. While Forepaugh's "rat-sheet" (right) calls Barnum's white elephant a fraud, his own elephant proved to be whitewashed.

great flowering with the Barnum and Bailey merger. It seemed that nothing was too gaudy or too sensational or too bright. The number and variety of acts multiplied almost beyond imagining. Costly gold leaf instead of paint or gilt covered the elaborate wood sculpture on hundreds of parade wagons, cages, chariots, and noisy steam calliopes.

But Barnum & Bailey was challenged by other circuses feeding the entertainment-hungry, expanding country of the eighties and nineties. Yankee Robinson was still a strong competitor. Pogey O'Brien owned or controlled more circuses than anyone else in history—except John Ringling, years afterward. For a brief period one of O'Brien's partners was Adam Foreback, a splendidly whiskered Phila-

TOO·WHITE·FOR·BARNUM

FOREPAUGHS·REPLY·TO·BARNUM

FOREPAUGH'S SACRED WHITE ELEPHANT

"LIGHT OF ASIA" PROVED BY THE HIGHEST·SCIENTIFIC·AUTHORITY TO BE GENUINE AND BARNUMS "SACRED WHITE?" ELEPHANT AND ALL ITS SURROUNDINGS A RANK FRAUD.

65

delphia butcher and horse dealer. Foreback changed his name to Forepaugh (shortened to 4-Paw) to suggest jungle cats. From 1866 until he died in 1890 Forepaugh had his own circus on tour and repeatedly nudged Barnum for supremacy.

Rat-sheet competition was bitter and very clever—as close to libel as legally possible. Electric lighting of circus tents was introduced in 1879, and thousands of spectators eagerly paid an extra fee just to look at the electric generators. One rival showman issued a rat-sheet denouncing the practice, insisting that the new Edison light "hurt the eyes . . . many [people] say they have not seen a well day since the exhibition. Persons predisposed to pulmonary complaints it will shorten their days and in many cases affect the tender brain of children. Look at their street parade, but don't go near the light at night or any other time. . . ."

On one occasion Barnum & Bailey advertised a street parade including 100 cages, 20 elephants, and hundreds of costumed people. Adam Forepaugh retaliated with a rat-sheet which insisted that the correct numbers for that procession were 23 cages, 14 elephants, and 25 mounted paraders in uniform.

In 1887 Forepaugh outwitted Barnum & Bailey by leasing Madison

New Life Grafted into the Old Oak (left) commemorates Barnum's 1881 merger. Barnum peers from the trunk, Bailey greets a Chinaman, and James Hutchinson holds a snake. The top-hatted man at right is still cross-eyed from watching a three-ring circus.

Square Garden for his New York opening, but Bailey persuaded him to agree to a joint opening of the two big shows at the Garden. The resulting program created a legend of magnificence for the Golden Age. There were sixty elephants and a glittering array of artists, the likes of which had never been seen before.

One cold November night that year, a big fire destroyed the Barnum & Bailey winter headquarters at Bridgeport, Connecticut. Leaping flames were visible for miles. All the wild animals except thirty elephants and a lion named Nimrod perished in the disaster. Nimrod was found in a barn, eating a calf. A farmer's wife, thinking he was a huge yellow dog, belabored the beast with a broom and nearly

Life, MAY 30, 1889

fainted when she learned the truth. One elephant survived by swimming in the dark, chilly waters of Long Island Sound. Within six hours after the fire, James Bailey had cabled the leading wild-animal dealer in Europe for animals to replace their loss.

In 1890 Adam Forepaugh died. Bailey and James E. Cooper bought the prosperous 4-Paw show and took it on tour to the west coast. Barnum, the master showman of them all, died on April 7, 1891. He had asked his wife to give him a simple funeral. "I've had enough shows and parades in my lifetime," he said.

The first great circus promoters were aging, dying, or going broke. In 1882 a long rainy spell and a train smashup in Illinois wiped out W. C. Coup's show, virtually ending one of the foremost circus careers of all time.

But new men were rising. From Baraboo, Wisconsin, in 1882, five young Ringling brothers set out hopefully on their first tour as showmen. There were seven Ringling brothers in all, but only Al, Otto, Alf T., Charley, and John attained the stature of master showmen and were pictured, each wearing a mustache, on the trade-mark of their circus.

Their initial tour in 1882 was made with the high-sounding title of Ringling Bros. Classic & Comic Opera Company. The modest program included skits, instrumental music, dancing, and singing. Later, after saving a few hundred dollars, the Ringlings went into the circus business. They bought some old wagons, fitting one with a canvas top, like a Conestoga wagon, for the advance agent. They even lettered it themselves to save a painter's charge of $11.40. They cut their own tent poles and stakes. They purchased lumber and made it into seat planks.

Al, who had once worked for Yankee Robinson, hired the aging showman as ringmaster. The show was called the Yankee Robinson & Ringling Bros. Great Double Shows, Circus and Caravan. Robinson added luster to the brave new venture but passed away before the first season closed. He literally died with his well-polished boots on, in his top hat and bright red coat, gallantly facing his audience at the very end. In the years that followed, the Ringlings never again put their family name second in the title of any show.

They opened in their home town on May 19, 1884, in a tent with two homemade poles, seating about six hundred people. The ring was merely a strip of red cloth staked out in a circle. There were no wild animals, not even a horse or a dog, just acrobatic feats, juggling, comic acts, an "educated" pig act, and tightrope walking, all to the blare of band music. The Ringling boys did most of the performing and even played in the band. They operated this mud show for six years before taking to the rails.

The deaths of Forepaugh and Barnum had left James Bailey as top man in the circus industry, but the brothers from Baraboo were coming up fast.

When the Barnum & Bailey show made a grand tour of Europe in 1897, Bailey left his other property, the Adam Forepaugh & Sells Bros. combined circus, to hold the fort in America. Forepaugh-Sells was ordered to invade the Midwest, which was Ringling territory, and provide stiff competition for the Baraboo boys. In 1898 the Forepaugh-Sells route book stated: ". . . Compared to the colossal magnitude of the Forepaugh-Sells show, all others are as waves of the sea, turbulent and impetuous, tossing over each other in a maddening stampede to check the onward, triumphal progress of the big show to victory's harbor."

The now gray-bearded Bailey led the Greatest Show on Earth through Europe with fabulous success for five years, returning to America in the late fall of 1902. His efforts to build up effective competition for the Ringlings, however, had failed to discourage them. Even before he began his European tour, the long red cars of the Ringlings had been parked on eastern sidings in Barnum & Bailey territory.

William Coup's candy-striped flying machine was probably more decorative than useful, for it was powered by a hand-cranked propeller. Coup's poster dates from about 1890.

James A. Bailey (right) ran the Barnum & Bailey circus after Barnum died. Then Bailey died in 1906, and the Ringling brothers bought the famous show and combined it with their own. It was said of the Ringlings (shown below with their parents) that they "became the circus kings of the world by adopting and observing the simple rule that it is better to be straight than crooked."

Back on his native soil Bailey met the new challenge head on. He had millions of dollars and he spent lavishly. He expanded his Big Top and menagerie tents by giving each half a dozen center poles. He built even more elaborate parade wagons. He opened his program with a cast of 1,250 persons in a great scenic spectacle called "Cleopatra." He paraded 260 superb horses, four abreast, around his sawdust-strewn hippodrome track. His show became so large that he needed ninety railroad cars to move it.

In advertising there was a terrific waste of time and material. Ringling crews and Barnum & Bailey crews followed one another around town and into the country with brushes and buckets of paste, tearing down rival posters or plastering their own over them. A choice spot might have as many as ten layers of competing paper, all pasted on top of one another within a few days' time. Now and then opposing crews came to blows.

Another trick was the use of a wagon that bore huge rat-sheets urging people to wait for the rival show, coming soon. If possible, this vehicle was thrust into a parade of the circus it denounced. If troupers saw it beforehand they would remove bolts or other parts so that it collapsed in the street. On one occasion Forepaugh-Sells held a free balloon ascension a mile away from where the Ringling matinee show was about to begin.

At length James Bailey signed a truce with the Ringlings whereby each show would play in nonoverlapping territory. While one toured the East, the other would be out West, and so on. In 1905 Bailey sold the Ringlings a half-interest in Forepaugh-Sells.

One day as Bailey was getting ready for his New York opening in Madison Square Garden, an insect bite caused an infection that ended his adventurous life on March 22, 1906. With the old maestro gone, the stock in Barnum & Bailey, Inc., dropped from five dollars to twenty-five cents a share. The Ringlings quickly bought the widow's half of Forepaugh-Sells, giving them complete ownership of that famous show. Then, on July 8, 1907, they purchased Barnum & Bailey. Buffalo Bill's Wild West Show went into the deal, but the Ringlings cared little for cowboys and Indians and soon sold it.

Al Ringling wanted to scrap the Barnum & Bailey title but the other four brothers outvoted him. They realized that those two names had a lasting appeal for circus fans everywhere. And so the 1908 season found the world's two biggest shows on tour again as usual, on different routes, but this time Otto Ringling was managing Barnum & Bailey.

Finally, in 1919, the Ringlings combined the two shows. The Greatest Show on Earth was at last christened with the magic name—Ringling Bros. and Barnum & Bailey.

Overleaf: This 1900 Barnum & Bailey poster, with dancing girls, elephants, and a harem, stresses the "weird wizardry of India and Arabia" that fascinated Americans of the era.
CULVER PICTURES

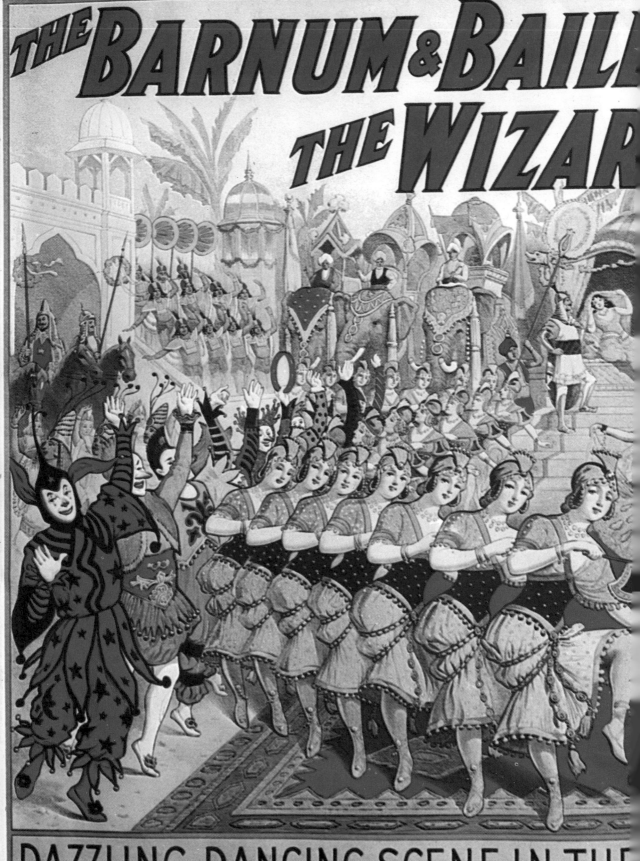

THE BARNUM & BAIL
THE WIZAR

DAZZLING, DANCING SCENE IN THE
COMBINING THE WEIRD WIZARDRY OF INDI

NEW BIG
INDO-ARABIC SPECTACLE
PRINCE OF ARABIA

AGICAL, MIGHTY, WORDLESS PLAY.

RABIA, IN OPULENT ORIENTAL GRANDEUR.

5.

Moving the Circus

Behind the tinsel, the excitement, and the promotion; behind the well-run, "no waits, no breaks" performances, were fearfully complicated schedules and long, weary hours of travel. Circuses became huge, but still they moved as if by magic from town to town over thousands of miles of country. No matter what the hardships, the feeding and living problems of the close-knit circus family, the public never saw them; the circus "saved a gallop for the avenue," and the band struck up the circus march on time.

In the early days, long before the time of Ringling Bros. and Barnum & Bailey, mud shows rolled from town to town by night, awakening villagers in the early morning with a shrill trumpet call to proclaim their arrival. They paid no license fee or ground rent, usually displayed only one small poster, had no elaborate costumes, and gave very few free passes. A full day's eating cost each man about twenty-seven cents. Many a tavernkeeper fed the troupe free for the pleasure and prestige of their company.

In 1828 nine men with seven horses constituted a large circus. Then Purdy

& Welch started its 1830 season on a scale previously unknown to American circuses, with twenty-four gray horses and a brass band of eight pieces in addition to other troupers and animals. This show hired roustabouts for the rough work of pitching tents, making the ring, and spreading the sawdust with shovels and rakes. Before, every trouper had had to help with such jobs.

Most circus travel was at night. Frequently the wagons creaked through mile after mile of lonely wilderness, their only light the torches carried by weary, plodding men or dim kerosene lanterns hung on wagons. Sometimes men would walk on ahead to plant flares at crossroads so the caravan would not lose its way. Although the average jump was only fifteen miles, they usually got started about three o'clock in the early morning darkness so as to arrive on time. Everybody was sleepy. Drivers nodded and musicians dozed on their seats in the band wagons, slumped over the instruments at their feet, with no shelter from the rain except their umbrellas.

The men and women lucky enough to journey inside closed wagons slept

Mud Show, *painted by Joel Salter, gives a glimpse of the grinding, weary toil required to move a show from one town to the next in the early days of the circus. Heavy wagons like this one as often as not bogged down in the muddy, rutted roads; bridges like that in the background were easily swept away by storms or flood waters, stranding the performers and animals.*

fitfully. Now and then a jittery big cat would scream. The huge patient elephants swished along in silence. If a wagon slipped into a ditch or became mired too deep for the horses to rescue, elephants pushed or hauled the vehicle back into the procession.

At times the caravan had to ford a creek. If the water was swift and deep, this called for real engineering skill. Sometimes a flood washed away a bridge or a rival show burned it, for competition was cruel. Too often the tired caravan had to turn back and take a long detour. On at least one occasion a wooden bridge broke under the heavy circus wagons, plunging human beings, animals, and equipment into the dark, cold water.

But no matter how rough the journey, no matter how tired they were, they pulled into town at a proud gallop. Wagon shows would halt beside a creek or pond where the performers would wash off the travel dust. Animals were watered. Parade wagons were cleaned; brasswork was shined. Flags, pennants, and the brightly colored plumes for the horses were taken out of storage chests and put in their places. Then, and not until then, would they move majestically into town.

In 1856 Spalding & Rogers decided on a revolutionary experiment. They moved a circus by the railroads that were slowly spreading over the country. Other circuses soon followed suit. The show people took planks into the cars and laid them across the seats to sleep on. Their rest might be broken two or three times a night, for whenever the train reached a junction point with a railroad that had wider or narrower tracks (there were many gauges in those days), the circus personnel, equipment, and animals had to be reloaded into another train.

During the first year of the Barnum-Coup circus in 1871, they toured New York State and New England in rainbow-hued wagons pulled by six hundred horses. The next season they took to the rails. Barnum reluctantly agreed to the use of the "steam cars" only after Coup convinced him that it would enable the show to skip the unprofitable small towns. Coup signed with the Pennsylvania Railroad and began loading at New Brunswick, New Jersey. They rolled southward in sixty-one colorful cars.

"You cannot possibly imagine the amount of labor involved," Coup recorded. "I never took the clothes off my back from the time of loading until we reached Philadelphia, our seventh stop! During all that time I was actually teaching the men the art of loading and unloading."

It was indeed an art at which Coup excelled. He devised the "piggyback" method of loading and unloading that every railroad circus has since copied. Detachable sheet-iron plates were laid between the flatcars to form an unbroken runway along their entire length, and an inclined ramp was set up at the end of the last car. Horses or elephants would pull the wagons up the ramp and along the runway, over the iron plates, to the first car. This was done with one wagon at a time until all the flatcars were filled.

The process was reversed at unloading time. Husky laborers, called razorbacks, eased the heavy vehicles down the ramp with the aid of ropes and brakes. Everything was done with military precision. In fact, while a big American show was touring Europe in the 1880's, the general staffs of both the German and the British armies studied Coup's system and adapted it to the transportation of artillery.

The "piggyback" method of train loading invented by William Coup is shown here. Roustabouts, called razorbacks, ease a wagon carrying tent canvas and poles off a flatcar.

Coup rented cars from the Pennsylvania Railroad for the 1872 season, but the rented equipment proved so unsatisfactory that he planned and had built new, longer cars of a standard height. Later on he had new wagons of greater capacity built in such a way that they would fit better on flatcars. Their wheels were made smaller, their bodies higher—but not too high to clear the railroad tunnels and bridges — and their lengths were changed to permit loading with no wasted space.

Barnum seldom rode in the same train as his manager. "If we both get killed, the show would be without a head," he said. One night the brilliantly painted train ran away down a

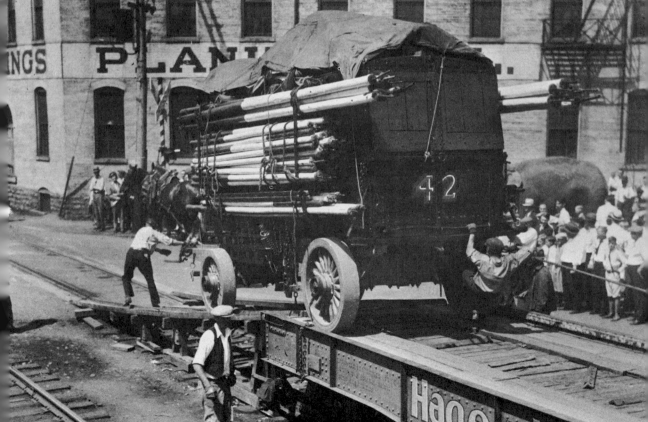

mountain grade in Pennsylvania and was nearly wrecked. After that, its cars were equipped with the newly perfected air brakes.

"Any boob can *run* a circus, but it's the wise showman who knows where to *put* it," a circus man once said. Circus routing was highly organized and could make the difference in a successful tour. The routers knew the country

Circus publicity began weeks ahead of time. These Barnum & Bailey advance men, shown mixing paste by the gallon, covered every available barn and fence with their posters.

as few other Americans did. One night in Ohio, as the train rushed through the darkness, someone asked John Ringling, as a joke, if he could tell where they were. Ringling is supposed to have raised the window, thrust one hand into the blackness, and said, "Fourteen miles east of Ada, Ohio, population, 2,465. Northwest corner of Hardin County — Farming town, but I've never made it though we showed Upper Sandusky — the town we just passed through — September 6, 1890, first season we had our show on the

rails. We'll be coming into Lima soon. Showed that town September 8, 1893, and July 21, 1894. . . ."

There were two ways to judge a circus—by the number of its elephants and by the number of its railroad cars. The big tent circuses owned all their cars but not the engines that pulled them. Each car was built much longer than standard railroad equipment—for one reason, railroad rates for hauling circus trains were based on the number of cars, not their size or weight.

At one time Barnum & Bailey oper-

ated five advance railroad cars that preceded the train by two weeks or more. Each carried a crew which put up posters, placed cards in store windows, mapped out parade routes, and arranged other preliminary details. Besides posters, paste, brushes, press releases, and blank passes, the supplies for advertising and publicity included a stereopticon for showing colored circus slides.

Technically, no circus had more than one train, but a big show usually divided its train into three sections.

CULVER PICTURES

It is not surprising that the circus train carrying the Greatest Show on Earth

BARNUM & BAILEY SHOWS

THE GREATEST SHOW ON EARTH

...AND ONE THIRD MILES LONG
WONDERS FROM EVERY LAND

deserved a poster of its own, for it was nearly as spectacular as the show itself.

The first section carried the cooks and their equipment; the horses; the ornate menagerie cages filled with wild beasts; the animal men, grooms, hostelers, blacksmiths, and roustabouts; and the lavish parade wagons.

Section two hauled canvas for the Big Top; wardrobe and horse tents; long wagons bearing tent poles, stakes, and knockdown seats for the grandstands; elephants and their handlers; ticket sellers and ushers; and lighting plants and the sanitation department.

The third section was made up of Pullman sleeping cars for the performers, the uniformed band, the executives, and the office personnel. It also carried the brightly-colored costumes. Usually, no meals were served on the train at any time, but snack bars provided light food. Top executives and center-ring stars had private compartments on the trains. The rest of the personnel were crammed two in a bunk, often three tiers high. Every inch of available train space was used.

A very few show owners occupied private cars, but the only woman performer to rate such an honor was the

Train wrecks posed a constant threat to the fast-traveling circus. They usually happened at night, when help was hard to get. This is the wreck of the Al G. Barnes train in 1930.

little blonde aerialist queen Lillian Leitzel, sometimes called the foremost circus star of all time. Her car even carried a piano, and she had a dressing room of her own on the lot, an almost unheard-of privilege.

The business of feeding people and animals was a very complicated matter in a big circus. Just before World War II, Ringling Bros. and Barnum & Bailey had 1,600 employees and a four-section train of 104 cars. They served 2,800 meals a day to their people, aside from feed for the animals. Every day the personnel ate, among other items, 226 dozen eggs, 2,470 pounds of fresh meat, 2,200 loaves of bread, 50 bushels of potatoes, and 2 large barrels of sugar. One husky canvasman ate 54 frankfurters at a sitting; another thought nothing of devouring a dozen pork chops at one meal.

So the circus rolled, lived, and was fed. Always at the end of the long journeys there was the unloading; the performers got ready to face the public, and the parade began!

On May Day, 1837, the Purdy, Welch & McComber circus advertised its wagon show by mounting the band on horses and two elephants and proceeding through the streets of Albany, New York, to the tootling of wind instruments and the thumping of drums. That was America's first circus parade. The parade flowered into magnificence during the Golden Age, until it became almost as important a part of the show as the performance itself.

One September morning when the Gil Robinson wagon show streamed into Lebanon, Tennessee, for a one-day stand, a murder trial was under way. Instead of lining the streets to view the circus, many citizens had gone into the courthouse to attend the trial. But Robinson decided to parade anyway. The noise of hoofbeats and rolling wheels, the shuffle of elephants, the occasional snarl of a lion, the ringmaster's shrill whistle, the murmurs and squeals from young bystanders, and the lively band music drifted into the drab courtroom through open windows. The judge could stand it no longer.

"It's no use, gentlemen," he said. "This court can't compete with the circus. The case stands adjourned till nine o'clock tomorrow morning."

In the fiercely competitive building of parade wagons during the Golden Age, thousands of dollars were spent on gold leaf and intricate carving. In 1846 the Isaac A. Van Amburgh show paraded with a band wagon described as "the largest ever seen on this continent." It was over twenty feet long and extended so high—seventeen feet from the ground—that its gilded canopy had to be lowered for passage under bridges. Barnum & Bailey's ornate band wagon, Two Hemispheres, was first shown to the public in 1903. This was a ten-ton vehicle, overlaid with gold leaf that cost forty thousand dollars. Forty horses, four abreast, pulled it, each horse with a nodding plume. The driver, Jim Thomas, sat atop the band wagon eighty feet be-

SALADDIN

P.P.P.

40

FORT
THIEV

PARADE SECTION
No. 10.

These floats—called tableau wagons—from Barnum & Bailey's "new million dollar free street parade" were designed to bring popular fairy tales to life for the children.

This 1903 photograph shows a forty-horse wagon team, once the pride of Barnum & Bailey's parade. The driver, Jim Thomas, controlled the forty matched bays by himself.

hind the lead horses, gripping ten reins in each powerful hand.

Adam Forepaugh's most famous wagon was a huge representation of St. George and the Dragon. The carvings were so enormous that men riding the wagon had to use long poles to raise overhead trolley and telephone wires. These carvings were fastened to a platform and lowered into the body of the wagon when not in use. In 1890 the Ringlings bought this great vehicle, removed its carvings, and converted it to a band wagon. The giant figures of St.

George, his horse, and the Dragon were installed on a cart pulled by zebras, donkeys, or ponies.

Another impressive Ringling feature was the bell wagon, with nine huge bronze bells in a setting of gilded wooden sculpture. Spring-operated levers were used to play tunes on this unique carillon during street parades. There were, of course, many other spectacular parade vehicles. Tableau wagons, some of them carrying scenes that telescoped up to thirty feet in height, presented ballet girls in fantastic costumes, historical subjects of all sorts, or Mother Goose stories. Barnum's gigantic, ornate orchestmelochor, somewhat like a calliope, pro-

duced harsh music that could be heard five miles away.

The steam calliope was patented and put to commercial use in 1855 by a man named J. C. Stoddard. It consisted of various-sized steam whistle pipes and a keyboard, usually mounted on a decorative wagon. Spalding & Rogers had one installed on their showboat *James Raymond* in 1857. As time went on, all of America's major circuses adopted this music.

In its early days the calliope, besides providing music of a sort, was used now and then to pump water into the dusty arenas, to wet overheated tent canvas on blazing midsummer afternoons, and even to serve as an emer-

The deafening music of the steam calliope always brought the parade to a close. Six elephants hauled this handsome calliope and its big steam engine through New York City.

gency fire fighter. Calliope players needed strong fingers and wrists to press the keys, and when the blistering hot whistles got out of tune they had to adjust them with wrenches.

"See the whole of my magnificent Street Parade. . . . It will take you an hour to see it through to the Calliope," Barnum promised in his circus posters of 1882. The calliope was always the sign that the parade was over. Its shrill whistles, heard for miles around, warned that it was time to hurry to the circus grounds for the big show.

87

6.

The Animal Acts

Man's most ancient victory over superior strength is the taming of animals. From the first touch of a human hand that gentled the fierce bull, calmed the wild horse and made it work, or soothed the collared leopard pets of ancient Egypt, this skill has been admired and even worshipped.

Young America was fascinated by the largest of exotic animals, the slow, ponderous elephants. To see these great beasts, with strength to push down trees and lift great weights, responding to the orders and gestures of their comparatively puny human trainers seemed to symbolize best the mysterious workings of the circus.

So strong was this impression that a new phrase came into the language. In nineteenth-century America "to see the elephant" meant to see and know the world, to be sophisticated; in effect, to have seen all there was to know of life.

Hachaliah Bailey's elephant, Old Bet, may have begun the craze, but she traveled over only a small part of the country. The elephant that became the greatest animal attraction in the country's history was P. T. Barnum's Jumbo. This enormous beast, weighing six and a half tons, gave a name to almost everything bigger than normal—Jumbo size.

Jumbo was not only the most-publicized animal of all time, but perhaps the best-loved as well. African elephants are traditionally harder to break than the more docile Indian species, which are somewhat domesticated and take naturally to training. But Jumbo, captured wild in Africa, was amazingly gentle. In his lifetime he carried thousands of children on his back in a howdah, or elephant saddle. Taken as a baby by a band of Arabs, he was sold in turn to the Paris Zoo, the London Zoo, and finally, in 1882, to the Barnum, Bailey & Hutchinson circus. When Queen Victoria and the distressed British people tried to buy Jumbo back and failed, the American ambassador, James Russell Lowell, summed up the controversy as "the

The animals were shown in a menagerie tent almost as large as the
Big Top. The Sells brothers' poster above promised zoological mar-
vels, beautiful birds, strange reptiles, and an African aquarium.

Overleaf: The gentle and much loved Jumbo, Barnum's most popular animal, carried thousands of children on his broad back. In this
poster he is made to look a good deal larger than he actually was.

P.T. BARNUM'S GREATEST SHOW ON EARTH

JUMBO THE PRIDE OF THE BRITISH ME

SANGER'S ROYAL BRITISH MENAGER

BARNUM, BAILEY & H

HE GREAT LONDON CIRCUS COMBINED WITH

Nº 88

ER MAJESTY, THE QUEEN. & OVER ONE MILLION & A QUARTER OF ENGLISH CHILDREN HAVE RIDDEN ON HIS
ER CHILDREN AND GRAND CHILDREN. BROAD BACK IN SEVENTEEN YEARS.

GRAND INTERNATIONAL ALLIED SHOWS.
SON. SOLE WNERS.

BARNUM'S AMERICAN DUNGEON

As Jumbo cries elephant-sized tears over his sale to Barnum, Britain's lion demands that America's eagle release him "in the name of Queen Victoria and over a million children."

only burning question between England and America."

Barnum, of course, saw to it that capital was made of the British feeling. Even before Jumbo arrived, all America knew about him from the newspapers. Barnum told a friend, "It was the greatest free advertising I ever heard of." Every day Jumbo consumed an average of two hundred pounds of hay; fifteen loaves of bread; a mass of oats, biscuits, onions, and fruit; five pails of water; and a quart of whiskey —and America was told all about it.

His keeper was English-born Matthew Scott, called Scotty. Man and beast were inseparable. They traveled in Jumbo's mammoth red-and-gold railway car, with Scotty occupying a high bunk in the rear. Sometimes the jolting of the car or the engine whistle made Jumbo nervous, and he would pass his long trunk over the bunk to make sure his friend was still there. A pat from Scotty's hand never failed to soothe him.

On September 15, 1885, when Jumbo was twenty-four years old, the circus pitched its tents on a vacant farm near the Grand Trunk Railway Station at St. Thomas, in Ontario, Canada. The long, glittering circus train was shunted to a siding, separated from the main track by only a narrow strip of cinders. That night thirty-two elephants were marched from the Big Top to be loaded before the evening show ended. The circus people confidently expected the main track to be clear for the loading, as the Grand Trunk Railway officials had promised. Thirty elephants had been loaded safely and were being fed. Last came Jumbo with a little clown elephant named Tom Thumb. Scotty escorted them. They were walking along the main track, lit flickeringly by kerosene flares, with band music from the performance in the distance filling the air, when an unscheduled freight train roared up behind them.

The engineer frantically blew his whistle and threw his wheels into reverse, but the engine rammed Jumbo against a circus car, derailing the locomotive, tender, and first car of the freight train. Jumbo was killed almost immediately. Telegraph, telephone, and the new transatlantic cable spread the sad news around the world. Publicity-hungry Barnum, wailing that he had "lost a million dollars," gave the newspapers a fantastic story about how Jumbo had sacrificed himself in order to save the little clown elephant.

Barnum hired taxidermists to stuff Jumbo's hide and mount his massive skeleton. He donated the stuffed hide to Tufts College near Boston and the skeleton to the American Museum of Natural History in New York. They are still there today; thus P. T. Barnum is still exhibiting the greatest elephant of all time.

Nature has equipped elephants with amazing brute strength. They have pulled many a huge circus wagon out of mud so thick that heavy Clydesdale draft horses could not budge it, and even tractors have bogged down. They have helped to load and unload trains, to switch boxcars, to raise and lower tons of canvas for the Big Top.

And they have shown themselves patient and dependable in crises. In 1882 the John Robinson circus was loaded onto a small narrow-gauge train for a trip through the Rocky Mountains to the mushrooming mining town of Leadville, Colorado. The track was steep and winding, with 560 curves in fifty-five miles. The top of the long grade was 10,200 feet above sea level, the highest point reached by any North American railroad. In rugged Kenosha Pass the engine stalled helplessly. Its driving wheels

failed to take hold even when the fireman poured sand on the rails, and the engineer kept the train from sliding backward only by slamming on the brakes. "All we need," the conductor said, "is a little extra push."

Then John Robinson called for the two elephants the train carried. The "bull handler" unloaded his pets, harnessed them together, and put them to work where a slip could mean death. The engineer released his brakes and opened the throttle wide while the fireman kept a wary eye on the steam gauge. It was a tense moment, but as the engineer said later, "The big boys jammed their heads against the rear end and up we went."

But sometimes elephant stability breaks down. In the late summer of 1926 a restless herd of Sells-Floto elephants set off to explore the majestic Canadian Rockies on their own. The harassed Canadian Pacific Railway

Barnum put out a highly romantic version of Jumbo's death: killed by a speeding freight train as he saved the life of his dwarf-elephant friend. The part about the train is true.

93

train dispatcher had to send out this unique order: "To all trains west. Keep lookout for elephants on track. Advise if sighted, from first telegraph office, giving location."

Elephants have a great sense of fun. One day in a little Iowa town the Cole & Walters circus had pitched its tents behind a schoolhouse, next to a playground. An elephant named Norma watched some children using the swings and slides. At length she went over, shooed them away with her trunk, backed up her big bottom to a swing, and tried her best to sit on it. Naturally, she could not make it, but she kept on trying, while the townspeople gathered around and howled with laughter. No wonder William C. Coup wrote in his autobiography, near the end of his career as a great showman, "I found the people almost as interesting as the elephants."

Like most circus animals out of their natural surroundings, elephants require a lot of care. Their skin is tender and must be rubbed with neat's-foot oil. They need the vitamin C that comes in fresh fruits and green vegetables, but captive elephants seldom get the fruit they crave unless they are sick—it is too expensive. For that reason, some of them will feign illness.

"Instead of feeding them peanuts and popcorn," wrote one handler, "zoo and circus visitors would do the elephants a real favor by giving them mellow ripe apples, oranges, grapes . . . or salad vegetables. But not peaches, which have large sharp stones."

The real animal basis of any circus is its troupe of well-trained, spirited horses. Some horses that work alone, or are ridden so that the attention of the audience is on the animal's performance instead of the rider's, are known in the circus as high school horses. This term comes from *haute école*, the French name for a method of schooling horses. The high school circus horse is taught tricks—waltzing, backward cantering, hesitating—all of which are foreign to his natural gaits.

One such animal, a stallion taught by the great trainer Joe Greer, could pick certain cards off a rack with his teeth as if in answer to numbers called by his master. Actually the stallion depended on human fingers for his cue. So sensitive was his nervous system that the movement of Greer's fingers one inch to left or right sent him to the correct card in the rack.

The same horse also rang chimes by pressing his nose on pads, becoming so proficient that he played the last three notes of one tune faster than Greer could give the cue.

The waltzing horses seem to have a musical sense as they dance around the hippodrome, but this effect is the responsibility of the band leader, who follows their movements so closely that their pacing leads him. The other performing horses, those dependable

The Ringling brothers' unusual brass quintet certainly appears to be working hard enough to sound like "a thousand human bandmen" as the poster claims, but the music they put forth was probably seldom "in time and tune."

whites that circle and circle at a steady gallop while the bareback riders dance and spin over them, are known as rosinbacks, because their wide, flat backs are rubbed with rosin to keep the riders' feet from slipping.

Of all the methods of controlling exotic beasts, the charming of great snakes is the most horrifying and fascinating. One of Barnum's posters showed a calm, bare-footed young lady wrapped in a huge reptile, with

The charms of the lady bareback rider are caught in this photograph taken at an unknown one-ring circus in 1905. Her reliable mount circles at a steady, clockwork pace.

the words: "Nearly a Mile of Writhing, Crushing, Hissing, Stupendous & Deadly Snakes. Huge Boa Constrictors, Gigantic Pythons, Dreadful Cobras, and Poisoned Saturated Vipers. The Defiant Hindoo Snake Charmer is seen Wreathed and Festooned in Their Awful Coils."

96

Snakes are really the most delicate creatures that travel with the circus. They are cold-blooded and shy. In very hot weather they have to be swabbed with warm water and have their mouths washed out. In cold weather they need warm blankets to curl up in, lest they die of pneumonia.

One of the most exciting moments at the circus comes when the steel cage is put around the center ring, with a barred passage leading from the menagerie tent. Then the lions, tigers, leopards, even black panthers, pad into sight. It is hard to believe that these big, sinuous cats can be tamed, yet there they are, pyramided on movable steps, elegant and polite. Wild and dangerous as they are (and they never cease to be), they respond to kindness.

Louis Roth, a trainer for Frank C. Bostock's Wild Animal Show, once nursed the lion Sultan when its leg was injured. One day in the steel-enclosed ring at Rochester, New York, Sultan killed a man. Roth entered the cage and quietly told the killer to drop its prey. Sultan obeyed and never again caused any trouble.

Roth had a way with wild creatures. He rode on Sultan's back; he taught a tiger to ride an elephant, although in the jungle those two animals are traditional enemies; and he even trained a leopard to ride a zebra, and three adult lions to ride a horse together. In 1910 he took charge of the menagerie in the Al G. Barnes show. An attractive little graduate nurse named Mabel Stark watched him at work. She was fascinated and soon gave up nursing to join the Barnes circus as an animal trainer.

This slim blonde came to love tigers, which she called "big striped tomcats." She was the first woman to break tigers, teach them tricks, and exhibit them in the ring. Her specialty was wrestling with a full-grown Bengal tiger, rolling over on the floor with him, and finally putting her face into his open jaws. One day she set an all-time record by entering a cage alone with sixteen tigers, unarmed except for a whip and a small chair.

Like all good trainers, Mabel Stark used patience and persuasion, never cruelty, in dealing with her pets. Without winning the animals' friendship, they cannot be trained. Unlike most trainers, Mabel never carried an iron fork or a revolver loaded with blanks to fire into the cat's face if necessary. She felt that the use of force only angers and confuses the animal.

An unaccustomed distraction can break the concentration between human and animal. Once in a street parade Mabel shared a rolling cage with four tigers, with only a stick for self-protection. The big cats were panicked by a runaway horse. One of them seized her leg and started to drag her toward the middle of the cage. Mabel beat off the savage attack with her stick and backed into the safety enclosure at the rear of the cage.

On another occasion she was in a steel-barred ring with a dozen striped

This 1895 poster shows liberty horses, which performed alone. They were trained to respond to the slightest change in their master's voice or the most subtle flick of his whip. At the upper left a liberty horse leaps through a fiery ring (a normal horse panics at fire); at the upper right another one gracefully walks a wire.

The lady obviously takes no nonsense from her leopards; the gentleman, on the other hand, scans his evening paper as if he had forgotten the house was full of lions.

The girl in the 1892 poster above might be the original "Sweet Flossy Farmer, the lovely snake charmer, who fell for a snake in the grass." The performing bears (above right) look woolly and comic, but they are among the most dangerous animals to train. The awkward look of the camels at right, from a 1900 poster, is also deceiving. They are capable of great feats of speed and endurance.

giants when the tent blew down, but with rare courage she kept them under control. She never came nearer death than in 1928 when she was with the John Robinson circus in a Canadian town. A drenching rain had made the ring slippery, and Mabel lost her footing. Two tigers sprang on her, one of them ripping open her left thigh. Only the intervention of a nearby lion trainer got her out alive.

A similar close call was experienced by the trainer Clyde Beatty. He slipped and fell to one knee. In a flash a tiger pounced on him. Then one of the lions in the same cage, which had long shown hatred for that particular tiger, took advantage of the opportunity to spring from its pedestal and claw the tiger. This diversion permitted Beatty to escape through a safety door.

In 1933, when Beatty was with the Hagenbeck-Wallace show, the wild beast menagerie was so large that it filled a nine-pole tent. Unlike Miss Stark, Beatty mixed his trained animals. One of his acts included a black leopard, two spotted leopards, lions, pumas, jaguars, polar bears, three brown bears, and three hyenas—all in the caged ring with Beatty at the same time.

Trainers can tell merely by looking at a big cat whether or not it is in an ugly mood, but the polar bear has a poker face and therefore is more dangerous and difficult to train. Brown bears have been taught to dance, to balance themselves on balls while holding parasols, to play musical instruments, to ride bicycles, and to roller skate. Some trainers even had bears driving motorcycles.

It is often thought that wild animals are drugged to calm them. They are not. If they were, they would not be able to walk, much less perform. The belief that wild beasts can be hypnotized by sheer will power is also fiction; nor do big circus cats have their teeth or claws extracted.

The giant gorilla Gargantua, the most publicized animal in circus history after Jumbo, was also the most ferocious. A veterinarian called him the least co-operative patient he ever had. No human being ever dared to enter Gargantua's air-conditioned cage or let him out for exercise or treatment. Every night the huge beast was given a new blanket. He would spread it out flat on the floor of his cage, without a wrinkle, and then sleep on it. Every morning, without exception, he deliberately ripped the blanket to shreds.

John Ringling North, boss of the big circus, feared that Gargantua might escape some day and kill any number of people. There was a standing order that if the mighty gorilla ever broke out of his cage, he must be shot on sight. "There isn't any way on earth to recapture him," North said, which was probably true. No adult gorilla, on the basis of known reports, has ever been taken alive in the jungle. (Gargantua was captured as a baby.) But Gargantua never escaped. He was twenty-two in 1949 when he died of pneumonia and infected teeth, fiercely

rejecting medical care to the very end.

Some animals have escaped. One day, shortly before World War II, when the big show was playing Madison Square Garden in New York, a female tiger broke loose, raced along a corridor, and knocked down a clown. Another clown, a dwarf named Paul Horompo, knowing that the lobby at the far end of the corridor was filled with children, jumped in front of the jittery big cat in an effort to head her off. The only weapon he had was a toy papier-mâché pick, but he slashed at the tiger with it. In surprise, the cat turned around and bounded back through the door from which she had come, and menagerie men caught her in a big net.

Later, when reporters interviewed him, the dwarf clown said: "Who's a hero? I was so scared I couldn't even whistle!"

Gargantua, the ugly-looking gorilla at left, had a temper that matched his looks. Not even the most patient trainer ever managed to make friends with him. Some trainers consider tigers, like the beautiful one above, the most dangerous of all the big cats to work with; they are likely to turn faster and strike with even less warning than panthers.

7.

On the Flying Trapeze

The most spectacular circus acts have been those in which human beings, caught in the tiny crossed beams of the spotlights, twirl in space above the darkened center ring, leaving the ground-rooted crowd gasping at their weightless grace. At the aerial act's climax the incessant brassy music stops and the whole Big Top is hushed.

The history of aerial acts goes back to the earliest acrobats who twinkled across the backs of galloping horses. As the years passed and daring increased, they performed higher on the slack wire, then even higher on the high wire; until finally at the top of the tent they swung from trapeze to trapeze with infinite grace.

Philip Astley, the trick-riding soldier in eighteenth-century London,

Within a decade after the Frenchman Jules Léotard had originated his act using a flying trapeze, the circus was filled with "daring young men" like the acrobats opposite, advertising an 1871 circus. The flying trapeze was the first innovation in centuries of circus tumbling.

J.W.HART. CIN.O.

Bird Millman (left) was a graceful and delicate low-wire artist of the 1920's and was already a headliner when she was fourteen. At the peak of her fame she married and retired from the circus.

Tiny golden-haired Lillian Leitzel (above) was not only a great performer but one of the best loved of all circus people. Here she does an end-over-end, one-handed turn known as the plange.

In 1859 Jules Léotard, the handsome young gentleman on the opposite page, took Paris by storm with his new trapeze act. He also invented the tights that are still worn by dancers today.

May Wirth, the Australian bareback rider posing with her horse at the far right, is generally considered to be the greatest woman equestrian. Her daring and stamina have never been equaled.

was the first circus equestrian acrobat; the greatest, however, was a lovely girl named May Wirth. Her contemporaries as well as the posters called her "The Greatest Bareback Rider that Ever Lived." She seemed to fly through her acrobatics as gracefully as a ballerina, her feet hardly touching the broad back of her galloping horse. Great courage and stamina, and years of training, made May Wirth the rider she was.

Back in 1856 James Robinson, the most famous equestrian of his day, had turned twenty-three perfect somersaults without stopping, all of them over a four-foot banner which his mount galloped under on each circuit around the ring. In the 1920's May Wirth became the only woman to do

the "back backward"—that is, she stood with her back to the horse's head and turned backward somersaults. Acrobatic performers never seem to remain satisfied with a trick that is already mastered. May Wirth improved on the back backward by tying baskets on her feet.

The somersault, which seems so simple on the ground, was the basic trick of the leapers, as circus people call those acrobats who catapult themselves into the air from a supple jump-up board and soar over the backs of massed animals or men. For years circus leapers were so popular that people would argue their merits as avidly as they now discuss modern baseball stars. But beyond the study and training of the best of the leapers

THE ADAM FOREPAUG
~AMERICA'S GREATEST

THE GREAT LIVINGSTONE, DAVENE & DE MORA TROUPE OF CHAMP SENSA

Despite their strenuous activities, the faintly smiling, formally dressed acrobats in this

AND SELLS BROTHERS
SHOWS CONSOLIDATED~

CROBATS, POSTURERS & HAND BALANCERS. THE WONDERFUL EUROPEA
MALE & FEMALE ARTISTS IN A PERFORMANCE ABSOLUTELY NEW TO AMERIC

1898 Forepaugh and Sells poster all have the look of department store mannequins.

TONY KARP, FPG

Etched in the spotlights, the aerialists spin and swing. Behind their perfect form are years of grueling training, first on the ground, later with a "mechanic" or safety belt, and finally with only a safety net seventy or eighty feet below. An unskilled landing in the safety net after a slip can mean a broken ankle or even a broken neck.

PHILIP O. STEARNS, PHOTO RESEARCHERS

NIAGARA LEAP BY THE WONDERFUL BUISLAY FAMILY

was a haunting and elusive ambition to do the triple—that "impossible" third somersault. So many leapers were killed trying to master the triple that the Italians christened it the *salto mortale* (death leap). A leaper named John Worland finally accomplished it in 1874 and made circus history. Years later Alfredo Codona mastered the triple from a flying trapeze into the arms of a catcher.

From the horse's back and from the jump-up board the acts soared higher. There are two kinds of wires for performers—the taut high wire, and the slack wire used lower over the center ring, which allows the performer to use the wire for leverage and spring. Bird Millman, the most popular wire-dancer of the twenties, was a graceful artist, the first American aerialist who did not use a balancing umbrella.

The supreme master of the high wire was Jean François Gravelet, better known as Blondin. On June 30, 1859, the slightly built Frenchman crossed Niagara Falls on a high wire three and one-quarter inches in diameter and about 1,200 feet long. For years afterward circus high-wire artists took the name of Blondin, and backdrops in the indoor circuses showed Niagara Falls as a background for daring.

The Wallendas also use the high wire. They have had as many as nine members of the family troupe on the wire at one time when they were performing for Ringling Bros. and Barnum & Bailey. Their program includes such dazzling feats as riding bicycles on a high cable three-quarters of an inch in diameter; and forming a human pyramid, three people high, and walking across the wire forty-five feet up, without the use of a net.

There were accidents, but usually the performers knew how to save themselves. The Wallendas had one of the more hair-raising mishaps when a guy rope attached to their cable gave way and the quartet, which was crossing as a human pyramid, lost its balance. The two Wallendas nearest the cable caught it with their hands, then caught their falling mates by extending their legs. They all hung on, miraculously, until a catch blanket to break their falls could be brought. But death caught up with the Wallendas in Detroit in January, 1962. Two of the troupe died as their human pyramid spilled from the high wires.

The only really new act to be developed in centuries of tumbling and acrobatics was originated by a young Frenchman named Jules Léotard. Up to the time of Léotard the trapeze had been a stationary bar; he turned it into

This mid-nineteenth century lithograph of the Buislay family act shows the effect of Blondin and Léotard on other aerialists. Painted on the backdrop is Niagara Falls, which Blondin had crossed on a tight wire. The aerialist in the center has modified Léotard's trapeze act, swinging across the theatre on two ropes.

the flying trapeze as we know it, and a new art of flying was born in the circus. But Léotard is remembered now not so much for his daring as for the costume he introduced, used by dancers and acrobats ever since.

After Léotard, the flying trapeze became the craze of daring acrobats. By the 1920's the equipment had grown into the great flying rigs used by Alfredo Codona and the amazing Concellos.

Alfredo Codona was a perfect stylist. His double and triple somersaults from the trapeze into the catcher's hands, his double pirouettes from the catcher back to the trapeze were all done with a supreme grace that has never been equaled. Arthur Concello also mastered the triple, and his wife Antoinette was the only woman ever to do it. Thus the Concellos could perform two triples on the same bill.

Sometimes a fall meant death—the only event that could stop a circus performance.

Tiny Lillian Leitzel was the most loved performer in the Greatest Show on Earth—loved not only by the public but by her fellow performers. She was only four feet eight inches tall and weighed less than a hundred pounds, yet when she walked into the center ring under the spotlight, she had the authority of a queen. When she went up the web (the rope that hangs from the roof to the floor), it was no normal climb. She rolled up smoothly and beautifully to the top of the tent, where two rings hung on short ropes from swivels. At the highest point under the roof, caught in the crossed beams of light and seeming as small as a moth, she did the plange, a one-handed swing, twisting herself over and over and over while the drums rolled in the darkness below. Every performance she did it from 75 to 100 times; her record at the plange was 249 turns.

In 1928 she and Alfredo Codona, both at the peak of their careers, were married. Just three years later, performing in Denmark, Lillian Leitzel plunged to her death when one of the swivels broke as she was doing a simple handstand on the rings.

As the circus grew bigger and bigger, the delicate techniques of such women as Bird Millman and May Wirth became obsolete. Grace was not enough — the public demanded more daring and spectacular acts, some of them easier to learn and perform than the triple somersaults and the wire-dancing. Defiance of death became less subtle, and in the process lost beauty.

When the height of the wires above the ring in this old poster is compared to the height of high wires in the modern circus, it is obvious how much more dangerous the acts have become. The lady at the top balances with her parasol while she tips coyly and confidently on one foot to reach for her handkerchief.

Circus daredevil acts were called "hair-raising" and "heart-stopping," and they usually were. Isabella Butler is the lady doing the Dip of Death at the top of the opposite page. Strapped into her early automobile, she raced down the inverted incline, shot across a forty-foot gap upside down, and landed safely and right side up. Schrever the Wonder (left) was typical of bicycle daredevils; he launched himself into space from a ramp as high as a ski run. The bicycle race above was held on an open-fence track five feet high and twenty feet in diameter. This sort of act was popular in the early years of the twentieth century when bicycle racing was a national sport.

119

Leonati, of the Forepaugh show, rode a high-wheeled bicycle down a narrow, vertical, spiral roadway fifty feet in height. No less daring was Mlle. D'Zizi, of Walter L. Main's circus, who rode a bicycle at a terrific clip down a long and steeply inclined runway that turned up at the bottom; she swept up and out across a fifty-foot gap, beneath which stood six elephants, and landed safely on another runway. "Spanning death's arch awheel," proclaimed a poster. "The bravest heart ceases to beat while this intrepid daughter of France soars toward the heavens."

Ernest Gadbin, billed as The Desperado, used to do a swan dive for Barnum & Bailey audiences from a platform eighty feet high. Landing chest first on a highly polished wooden slide, he would zoom down and then shoot up into the air, finally coming to rest in a net. A woman daredevil in the same show, Isabella Butler, was featured in the Dip of Death. In the early days of the twentieth century, when the automobile was devilish anyway, and boys still shouted "Get a horse" at tentative drivers, she drove a small, primitive car down a very steep runway. At the end of the ramp the car turned upside down and hurtled (according to her billing) "into space forty feet away across a veritable chasm of death," righting itself as it landed on a second runway and sliding down it to a stop.

Another feature of the Barnum & Bailey show was a spectacular human cannon ball act performd by Zazel, an English girl whose real name was Rosa Richter. Wearing pink tights, she curtsied to the crowd as she entered the mouth of a wooden cannon and rested her feet on a tiny platform inside, beneath which were strong springs. Her partner set off a charge of gunpowder. At the same instant he released the springs, and Zazel was shot out of the cannon through the air for a distance of about seventy feet, falling into a net.

Hugo Zacchini revived the human cannon ball act in 1929. His monster machine, developed by his father in Italy, shot him, by compressed air, over 70 feet up and across 135 feet of space at a speed of eighty miles an hour; the machine gave off smoke and a true cannonlike blast.

Stunts of this sort, spectacular as they are, really belong to the side show. It is when the drums roll and the crowd is silent and tense that the circus is at its best, for then the "daring young man on the flying trapeze" goes into his act.

The modern high-wire artist at right, using a parasol for balance, dances high above the center ring. She dresses in a tutu and walks the wire on the tips of her shoes like a ballerina. Such acts add the dimension of grace and beauty to traditional circus daring.

8

Bring on the Clowns!

This 1856 poster is one of the finest to have survived. Most traditional clown garb appears here, including jesters' costumes, pointed caps, and grotesque face make-up. The clown at far right adds a touch of patriotism with his starred and striped tights.

LIBRARY OF CONGRESS

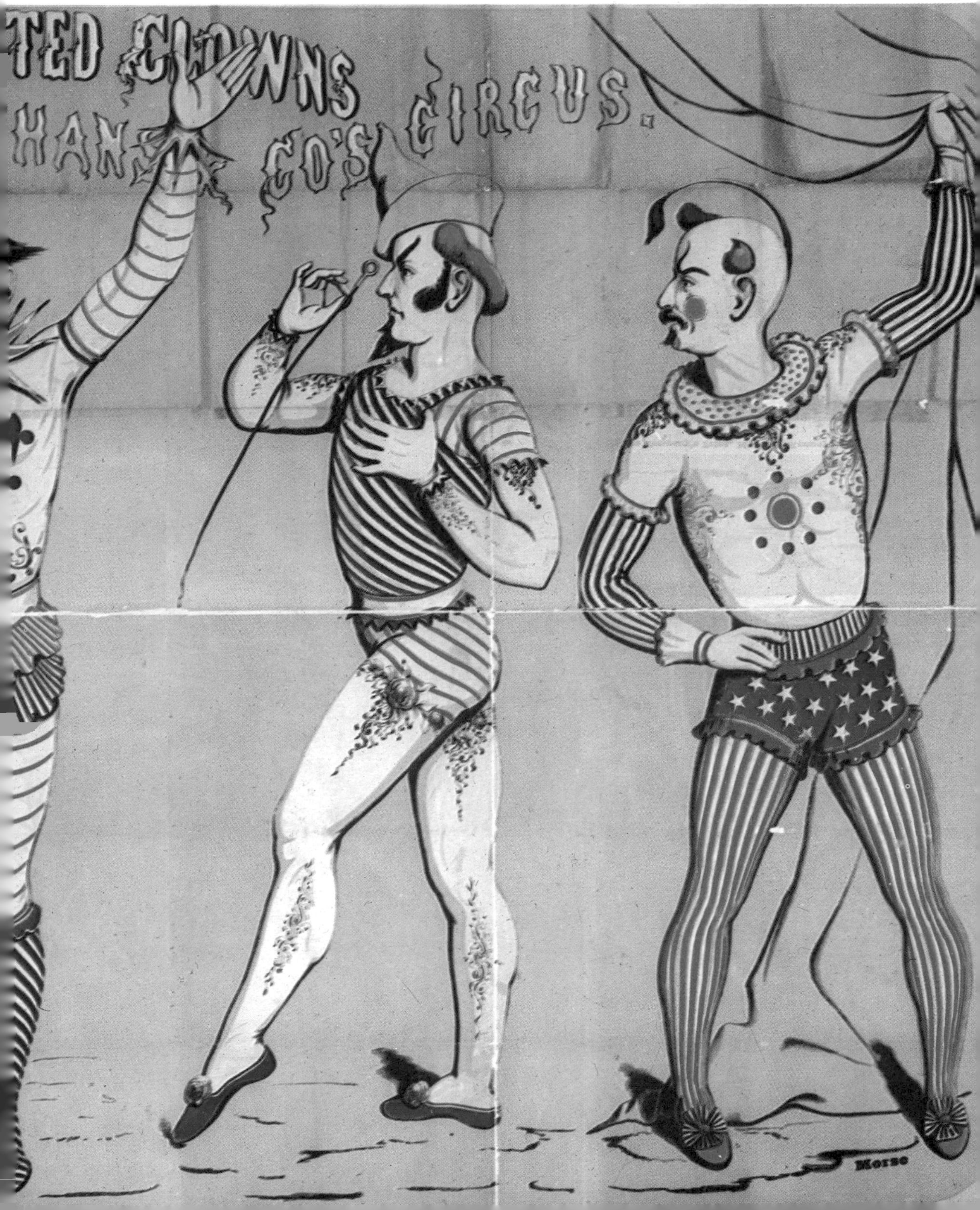

If the wild animals provided a touch of the exotic, and the aerialists a touch of daring, the clowns brought the final touch of laughter to make the circus of the Golden Age the great entertainment it was.

From the Grand Entry to the Grand Finale, the clowns were everywhere. Dozens of them marched and performed in the clown walk-around between acts; others, known as carpet clowns, circulated through the audience, and many a child was pleased and scared when the carpet clown singled him out for a joke. They seemed to interfere with everything that was going on, from awkwardly helping the property man to standing by hopefully with a frying pan while the seal trainer tossed fish to his seals as a reward for their obedience. They hit each other with huge sausages, they sprawled flat on their faces, they stumbled into tanks of water, they fell off everything they tried to climb onto.

Yet all the time they seemed to play the fools, the clowns performed a service vital to the smooth running of the circus. They filled in as the acts were changed, diverted the audience from the work of the property men, and kept the circus going at its "no waits, no breaks" pace.

As with their ancestors, the jesters

Joey Grimaldi, shown performing in London in 1811, was not only the first important circus clown, but also one of the best. Clowns are still called joeys in his honor.

of medieval courts, nothing was sacred or safe from their ridicule. Whenever anything, even a dangerous act, was taken too seriously, there was a clown to poke fun at it. Amidst all the daring, speed, and danger, they provided the release of laughter.

There are two basic kinds of clowns in the circus. The first is the classic zany, or fool. His white face, huge red spots, pompons, pointed hat, and great baggy trousers came originally from the *Commedia dell' Arte*. This was a group of strolling comic players that toured Europe for centuries, playing familiar stock characters at fairs or in village squares or wherever they could gather an audience. Of these characters, Harlequin—always a thief, always in love, always in trouble, and always just able to get himself out of his scrapes—was most like the modern bewildered but wily clown.

The second kind of clown is called the august clown; he always dresses or acts pretentiously and then loses his dignity. There are several stories about the origins of this act. One version has it that at the Renz circus, performing in Berlin in the 1860's, a young rider named Tom Belling was amusing himself by dressing in the clothes of a stable boy, which were much too big for him. He heard the circus owner approaching; knowing his fearful temper, Tom ran blindly and suddenly found himself in the ring. Trying to get out of his baggy clothes, he fell down, and the audience, thinking it part of the act, shrieked with laughter.

In nineteenth-century America mules were considered the most comical of animals, and they were featured in many early circus acts. These scenes show the "educated" mules Pete and Barney as they appeared in Dan Rice's circus, probably sometime in the 1850's.

MR MYERS AS CLOWN.

From that day on Tom Belling remained a clown, and out of his act grew the caricature of a seedy English gentleman—awkward, usually weaving and red-nosed with whiskey, trying hard to help but getting himself into more and more difficulties. Charlie Chaplin's little man is of this type; so is Emmett Kelly's tramp.

The first clown to become a star and make clowning a special act was Joey Grimaldi, who was the idol of London in the early nineteenth century. He made people laugh at themselves as few clowns have since. At the height of the romantic revival, when it was fashionable to die, or at least get sick, for love, Grimaldi had the whole of London singing a heart-rending song called "The Oyster Crossed in Love," which he sang to a huge oyster before putting it out of its lovesick misery by eating it.

In the middle of the Napoleonic Wars, when the British were at their most patriotic, he teased them by dressing as John Bull (the British equivalent of Uncle Sam) or as "The Bold Dragoon," with coal scuttles for boots, imitating the military strut of the cavalry dragoons. No London character, from chimney sweep to dandy, was safe from Grimaldi's wit. In one act he was a poet who sat in his lonely

A typical example of the circus clown known as the zany is shown at left, from an 1856 poster. Dan Rice (right), the first great American clown, was so popular that his salary was much larger than the President's.

Clowns often employed "educated" pigs and monkeys as well as mules in their routines. This handsome Barnum & Bailey poster of the 1880's is an example of a common circus advertising technique. While it appears that there were three of these clown-pig-monkey acts in the show, there was actually only one such act; what is shown is three different parts of the same performance.

attic, singing about love and accompanied by roof-top cats until the room got so hot from his passion that it caught fire. He became so famous that to be a clown was to be called Joey; circus clowns have been called joeys ever since in his memory.

Many clowns have been talented tumblers or riders. Philip Astley hired a clown to tease and imitate his serious acts; he was to make a wild, awkward dash around the ring in a comic routine called The Tailor's Ride to Brentford.

In America, The Tailor's Ride to Brentford became the Pete Jenkins act, named for a backwoods bumpkin character, Pete Jenkins from Mud Corners, created by the nineteenth-century clown Dan Rice. The ringmaster would make an announcement that the equestrian was unable to appear. A seedy-looking yokel, slightly the worse for drink, would weave his way out of the audience and shout "Fake," and the annoyed ringmaster would challenge him to ride instead. Ride he would, spilling off the horse, chasing it, grabbing its tail to hang on, shedding clothes in his maniacal effort until he emerged as a graceful equestrian, spangled tights and all, and finished the act in a blaze of true riding tricks.

A well-known version of the Pete Jenkins act was that of "Poodles" Hanneford. An expert rider, he shambled foolishly into the ring wearing an oversized collegiate coonskin coat and a derby that looked like it had been to too many parties. He would mount a seemingly bad-tempered, balky horse like a tenderfoot and fall off it over and over as it galloped wildly around the ring.

No matter how often the Pete Jenkins act is done, people can almost always be fooled by it. As late as the 1950's, at the Mills brothers' circus in London, a solemn-looking, correctly dressed English gentleman, newspaper tucked under his arm and rolled umbrella in his hand, would walk sedately into the ring despite the protests of his embarrassed wife and accept a challenge to ride a mule. The Pete Jenkins act was on again, and the audience laughed as hard as ever.

As the clown acts became more popular, the funniest animals in American folklore, mules and pigs, were trained to become part of the show. The most famous pig of them all, a purebred American razorback, was known as Lord Byron. Lord Byron belonged to Dan Rice, who entered the circus business in 1840. Rice taught Lord Byron to answer questions by grunting at the right time and to spell easy words by nudging the correct letter cards with his snout.

The tall and lanky Rice grew a beard, dressed in red and white stripes like the American flag, and called himself Uncle Sam, the new symbol of the young democracy. He had the same genius for revealing Americans to themselves that Joey Grimaldi had had with the British.

In that vigorous era the nation was

Torrey Brothers, Printers, 13 Spruce Street, New York.

In this 1872 poster the clowns are a featured main act. The one at the right sings, the three at the upper left mimic a tumbling act (many clowns are trained acrobats), and the one in the center kicks his hat onto his head. As the adult clowns poke fun at the serious circus acts, they in turn are taunted by the child clowns.

growing and flexing its muscles, and Americans felt they had to work hard or go under; Rice lampooned this attitude with a song called "Root, Hog, or Die." Uncle Sam and Lord Byron would seesaw together or walk around the ring with the pig weaving a figure eight in and out around his master's legs. As a finale, Rice offered the pig a boxful of assorted flags. Lord Byron invariably chose the Stars and Stripes and waved it in his jaws while Rice sang "Root, Hog, or Die."

Rice was more than a clown. He was a slack-wire artist, a jig dancer, an equestrian, a circus manager, a professional strong man, and an animal trainer. With infinite patience, he even trained an Indian elephant named Lalla Rookh to walk the tightrope. He also had an enviable reputation on the frontier for being able to lick any man he fought.

Circus owners bid high for his services (as much as $1,000 a week during the Civil War), and Rice switched from one to another. For about twenty years he played river towns by steamboat, pitching a tent ashore at each boat landing, often with his own show, but sometimes backed by Spalding & Rogers. The sight of mighty Dan Rice leading his street parade on a summer morning at McGregor, Iowa, is said to have inspired the Ringling brothers to become showmen. In 1884, when the Ringlings began trouping, they copied Rice by having an "educated" pig as one of their major attractions.

With all the standard costumes and acts of clowns, they each have an individual trade-mark—their modification of the classic make-up. Even though their faces are painted white, no two clowns have the same facial pattern, whether it be the joey's grinning, white face streaked with bright color, or the unshaven, sad hobo's face of an august clown like Emmett Kelly, the most famous modern American clown. Even though they might enter the Big Top many times during the course of a performance, and in different costumes, their facial make-up never changes. In the dressing tent they stay together in a section called clown alley. Before a performance, rows of them can be seen carefully drawing on the faces by which they are known, and which each clown guards jealously.

"Clowns are pegs to hang circuses on," P. T. Barnum said. In the more intimate days of the one-ring circus they did main acts; there were many talking or singing clowns like Dan Rice. Johnny Robinson composed many songs and climbed a rope ladder to sing them in a loud voice that reverberated all through the tent. Some clowns were fine acrobats. Bob Sherwood, who got his start with Dan Rice's show, was billed as the Champion Clown Acrobat of the World. One of his stunts was to turn a double somersault over two elephants and six horses. Clown tightrope walkers, who must lurch and weave across the tightrope in baggy pants, seeming to fall and just barely managing to recover their balance, are actually among the most highly trained wire walkers.

As the circus grew to three rings and the Big Top got bigger and bigger, the days of the talking or singing clown ended. He went back to his most ancient ancestor, the cavorting mime of Greece and Rome who depended on broad, slapstick humor. Anything was tried for a laugh—gigantic shoes, wired-on skunks, three-foot cigars, grotesque masks, bare feet made of papier-mâché. On his chest Paul Jerome wore a heart-shaped neon light which flashed on and off with joy whenever he met a girl. Some clowns have pet dogs trained to snap at their padded rear ends, billy goats to butt them, waddling ducks, or dogs fixed up to look like miniature horses or elephants. Tiny chugging clown cars drive into the arena, and clown after clown after clown climbs out, enough to fill a bus. There are clown bands, clown fire departments, and clown weddings.

One act as old as the *Commedia dell' Arte* is the elopement. A ladder is put up to a false window, and a clown climbs it. His love hands him her suitcase, then a bird cage, then a chair, a table, a skillet. Up and down the ladder he goes, until he is exhausted and household goods of all sorts are piled on the ground. Finally, as he climbs up for the last time to claim his bride, an irate clown father appears instead in the window and tips the ladder over.

While all these acts are done at zany speed between the main acts of the circus, the carpet clowns circulate

These modern clowns demonstrate the variety of comic faces evolved from the basic white-face make-up. A clown may change his costume during a performance, but never his comic mask. It is his individual trade-mark, and no two are ever exactly alike. One thing they do have in common: their grins can be seen all the way across the Big Top or the arena.

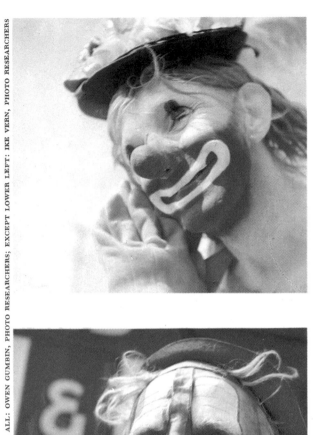

through the audience. In the mid-nine-teenth century, Bob Sherwood was clowning around the arena in London. He stopped beside the royal box and held out his hand to Queen Victoria. Court attendants gasped. But the Queen graciously took his hand and the audience cheered.

Years later, Emmett Kelly strolled around the same arena in his role of Weary Willie, the white-faced hobo, dejectedly nibbling a loaf of bread. He sat down on the tanbark in front of Kay Stammers, the young British tennis champion, and gazed up at her as if he were hopelessly in love. A few minutes later, resuming his stroll, he offered the Lord Mayor of London a piece of his bread. Londoners gave him a great ovation.

There is none of the slapstick in Kelly's performance. He pretends to sweep away a pool of spotlight that keeps dogging his steps. He blows up a toy balloon until it bursts and then buries it pathetically in the sawdust as a child would bury a dead bird. He opens up a peanut with a sledge hammer and seems bewildered because it is ground to powder.

As a rule, clowning is taboo while stars are performing in the rings. But now and then a featured artist asks a clown to give a comic touch to his or her act. Kelly would prop a ladder against a horse ridden by the famous equestrian Lucio Cristiani, then climb the ladder and carefully sweep off the horse's back with a broom. Just before a popular wire walker entered the ring, Kelly used the wire as a clothesline for his ragged bandana and other bits of shabby clothes until the acrobat appeared and chased him away.

Although the clowns hang on to their individuality as much as they can, and a rare genius like Emmett Kelly can become a star with his many routines (he once said that he appeared in every act but the all-girl aerial ballet), they no longer have the starring main acts they did in the days of Grimaldi and Dan Rice. The huge tents destroyed their intimacy with the audience.

By the 1930's the Greatest Show on Earth had over a hundred clowns. At the clown walk-around they seemed like a regiment; delicate satire was overwhelmed by sheer size.

But there were times when a single beautiful gesture could epitomize clowning. As the climax of the performance of Burr Robbins' circus in the 1880's, all the spangled acrobats of the company lined up; in turn they ran up the jump board and turned spectacular somersaults over the backs of massed horses, elephants, and camels. At the end came the clown Pete Conklin. He ran after them to the edge of the leaping board, paused, and gently, over the long line of animals, tossed his hat.

Sad-faced Emmett Kelly is the greatest modern American clown and one of the greatest clowns of all time. Kelly makes use of pathos as well as satire, and his character of Willie the Tramp is known all over the world.

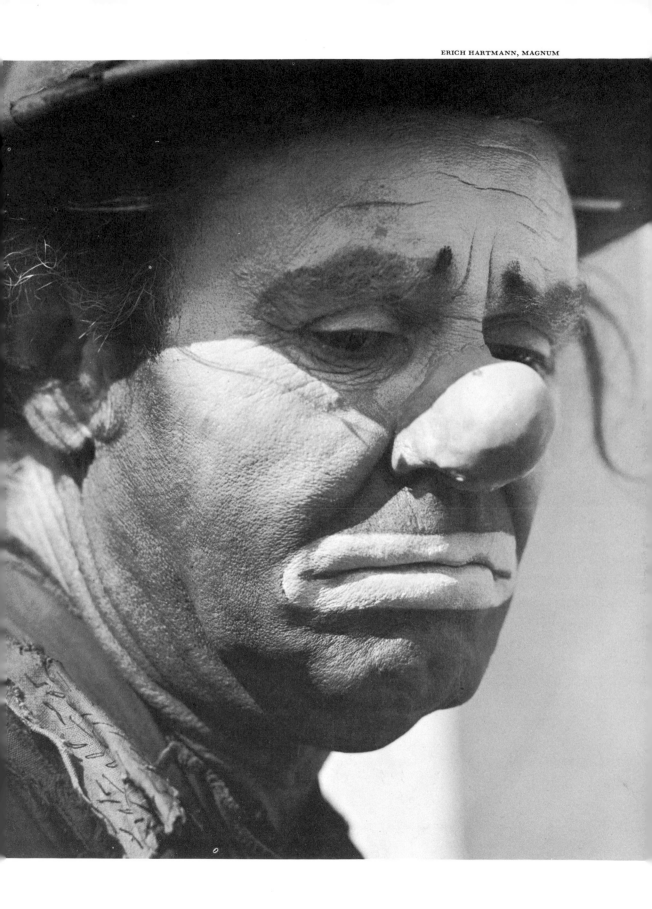

9.

Grand Finale

There is much of the nostalgic appeal of the old-time traveling show in H. J. Soulen's painting called Circus Tents. *On the vacant muddy lot is the tent city, main poles sharp against the dark sky, canvas ghostly in the moonlight, wagons parked ready for the parade. By next dawn the show will be off for yet another one-day stand, and the lot will be empty once more.*

On July 16, 1956, John Ringling North, president of Ringling Bros. and Barnum & Bailey, made an abrupt announcement to the American press. Putting the end of the Golden Age into words, he said, "The tented circus is a thing of the past." The Big Top would come down on the show to which P. T. Barnum had given his showman's instinct and James Bailey his organizing genius; the show that William Coup had taught to travel and the Ringling brothers had expanded to its zenith in the 1920's.

The circus world was stunned at North's announcement. The Big Top had survived so much. The Depression had closed many shows. Any number of brightly painted circus cars were left to rust on sidings, and circus winter quarters became ghost towns. But Ringling Bros. and Barnum & Bailey never closed.

In 1944, at Hartford, Connecticut, disaster nearly destroyed the Greatest Show on Earth. Twenty minutes after the performance began, the Big Top suddenly burst into flames. The most daring high-wire family of all, the Wallendas, was in mid-air; the shrill whistle of the ringmaster brought them down. Ringling's band leader, Merle Evans, struck up the traditional disaster alert, "The Stars and Stripes Forever." The audience panicked; 168 people were killed and 487 others seriously injured. The Ringling management paid nearly $4,000,000 in damage claims. After the Hartford fire circuses were permitted to fireproof their

The people shown in the photograph at right are fleeing the American circus' worst disaster. On July 6, 1944, fire ravaged the Ringling Bros. and Barnum & Bailey show in Hartford, Connecticut, killing 168 persons.

Below, the show is over. The audience has gone, the floodlights have dimmed; with a sigh of canvas, the Big Top comes down. In 1956 the Greatest Show on Earth struck its tents for the last time and moved indoors.

JERRY COOKE

tents with chemicals that had been restricted to military use.

But depression and disaster did not end the Golden Age. Throughout its history the circus had survived other depressions and fires, as well as train wrecks, floods, and hurricanes. What had happened was that the circus itself had changed, and the America it entertained had changed too.

Ringling Bros. and Barnum & Bailey had simply grown too big for its canvas. It was no longer profitable to tour with the enormous Big Top, the kitchen equipment that fed 1,500 people, the complicated and expensive lighting plant. Empty lots large enough and near enough to the centers of towns and cities became harder to find. The only answer was to go indoors. And indoors, even though the acts could be bigger and the high wires even higher, something of the dreamlike, here-to-day-gone-tomorrow quality was gone.

Perhaps as important, the American way of life had changed. In the Golden Age the circus was unquestionably the greatest show on earth; nothing else could touch it. It was, in short, America's foremost entertainment. But the country grew and the roads became crowded, and by the 1930's the parade, a major part of Circus Day, was gone. The gaudy circus poster went almost unnoticed amidst the welter of highly colored, eye-catching advertising signs. Other forms of entertainment—radio, movies, and, after World War II, television—began to compete with the circus. It was no longer the greatest show on earth, and when that happened, some of the magic of Circus Day disappeared.

If the fabulous era of the circus has faded, the circus itself is certainly very much alive. John Ringling North made one mistake. He talked about tent shows in general, when what he really meant was his own. For the American tent circus is making a comeback. In 1962 more than half the country's thirty-seven circuses are performing under canvas. Their tents rise as they always did. Most of them arrive now in gaudy truck caravans, with decorated trailers instead of the slow, trundling wagons of the mud show days. The Hunt brothers' circus, the oldest in the country under continuous family ownership, pitches a Big Top 110 feet by 170 feet.

Most of the finely evolved circus acts are still to be seen. High flyer Fay Alexander does a triple somersault from the trapeze, and acrobats "soar from spring-board runs over the backs of massed elephants." The Wallenda family forms its amazing human pyramids on bicycles balanced on the high wire at the top of the tent, and Clyde Beatty enters the steel cage with his "huge jungle group of Royal Bengal tigers and black-maned Numidian lions."

Shown here is the human pyramid act of the Wallenda family, the finest modern high-wire troupe. Relying on long balancing poles, they work forty feet up, usually without a safety net. They also do the act on bicycles.

America has even produced one of the great circus stars, after depending almost entirely on foreign-born stars for so long. Jean Mendez is considered the most fearless high-wire artist in the world today. He began his training in a Brooklyn YMCA and went on to be schooled by Karl Wallenda, head of the Wallenda troupe.

To capture the memory of Circus Day, museums have been set up in famous old circus towns. The pioneer circus museum at Somers, New York, where Old Bet is buried, commemorates the Cradle of the American Circus. Two museums at Sarasota, Florida, former winter quarters of Ringling Bros. and Barnum & Bailey, have collections from the Golden Age of the Barnum & Bailey and Ringling broth-

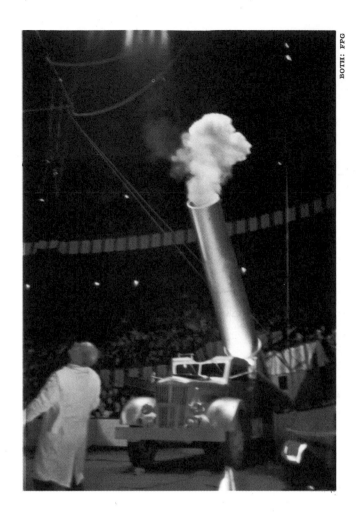

Few circus acts are as spectacular as the one above. A truck carrying a huge cannon lumbers into the center ring; slowly the barrel is raised. At the signal there is a puff of smoke and a clap like thunder, and the human cannon ball soars high into the air and lands, finally, in a net.

At left is the splendidly outfitted ringmaster, known in circus parlance as the equestrian director. While he appears to be only an announcer, he is actually directing the whole complicated performance. His whistle keeps the acts moving and on cue; in the center ring his word is law.

Amusement Business

ers merger. There are also museums at Baraboo, Wisconsin, home town of the original Ringling brothers, and at Peru, Indiana, home of several circuses in the past. There are even plans to set up at Venice, Florida, the last Big Top used by the Greatest Show on Earth as an exhibition of.Circus Day as it once was.

If the circus is no longer the great-

est show on earth, it is nevertheless very good entertainment. Whether under canvas or inside an auditorium, when the webbing is hung, the sawdust put down, the painted rings set up, the hippodrome raked smooth for the Grand Entry, something of the magic returns. The band strikes up "The Entry of the Gladiators." The aerialists whirl high above, and shouts

of "peanuts—popcorn" mingle with the crowd's roar. A balloon slips out of a child's hand and floats free and bright to the roof. The elephants do their solemn, patient dance in the center ring. The clowns tumble, cavort, and fight their way around the hippodrome. Astounding acts follow one upon another at a "no waits, no breaks" pace. The circus is back in town!

The fortunes of the circus may change over the years, but the faces of children watching always remain the same. Its magical blend of amazement, excitement, and suspense is captured in this photograph taken just at the moment when the human cannon ball was fired.

As long as there are dancing elephants and daring aerialists and an audience to thrill, the circus will go on.

The intricate carving on this old parade wagon shows St. George slaying the dragon.

AMERICAN HERITAGE PUBLISHING CO., INC.

BOOK DIVISION

Editor
Richard M. Ketchum

———— * ————

JUNIOR LIBRARY

Managing Editor
Stephen W. Sears

Art Director
Emma Landau

Assistant Editors John Ratti · Mary Lee Settle

Picture Researchers Julia B. Potts, *Chief*
Dennis A. Dinan · Judy Feiffer · Mary Leverty

Copy Editor Patricia Cooper

ACKNOWLEDGMENTS

The Editors are especially indebted to Leonard V. Farley, librarian of the Harry Hertzberg Circus Collection, San Antonio Public Library; Charles P. Fox, director of the Circus World Museum, Baraboo, Wisconsin; and Paul Vanderbilt, curator of the Wisconsin State Historical Society, for their generous assistance and counsel in locating pictorial material. In addition, they wish to thank the following individuals and organizations for their assistance and for making available pictorial matter in their collections:

American Antiquarian Society, Worcester, Mass.—Clifford K. Shipton

Chicago Historical Society—Mrs. Mary Frances Rhymer, Bruce Smith

John Durant, Longboat Key, Fla.

Colonel Edgar Garbisch, New York

Harvard Theatre Collection, Cambridge, Mass.—Audrey Hosford

Irwin Kirby of *Amusement Business*

Library of Congress—Virginia Daiker

Museum of the City of New York—May Seymour

New-York Historical Society—Paul Bride, Betty J. Ezequelle

Ringling Museum of the Circus Sarasota, Fla.—Mel Miller

FOR FURTHER READING

Bradna, Fred, and Spence, Hartzell. *The Big Top: My Forty Years with the Greatest Show on Earth.* Simon and Schuster, 1952.

Clarke, John Smith. *Circus Parade.* Scribner's, 1936.

*Cooper, Courtney Ryley. *Boss Elephant.* Little, Brown, 1934.

Cooper, Courtney Ryley. *Under the Big Top.* Little, Brown, 1923.

Desmond, Alice Curtis. *Barnum Presents General Tom Thumb.* Macmillan, 1954.

Dhotre, Damoo Gangaram, and Taplinger, Richard. *Wild Animal Man.* Little, Brown, 1961.

*Duncan, Thomas W. *Gus the Great.* Lippincott, 1947.

Durant, John and Alice. *Pictorial History of the American Circus.* Barnes, 1957.

*Edell, Celeste. *Here Come the Clowns.* Putnam, 1958.

Fox, Charles P. *A Ticket to the Circus: A Pictorial History of the Incredible Ringlings.* Superior Publishing Co., 1959.

Hamid, George A. *Circus.* Sterling Publishing Co., 1950.

Kelly, Emmett, and Kelley, F. Beverly. *Clown.* Prentice-Hall, 1954.

*Fiction

Knecht, Klara E. *The Circus Book.* Saalfield Publishing Co., 1934.

Lewis, George, and Fish, Byron. *Elephant Tramp.* Little, Brown, 1955.

May, Earl Chapin. *The Circus from Rome to Ringling.* Duffield & Green, 1932.

Moses, Horace S. *Here Comes the Circus.* Houghton Mifflin, 1941.

Murray, Marian. *Children of the Big Top.* Little, Brown, 1958.

Newton, Douglas. *Clowns.* Franklin Watts, 1957.

North, Henry Ringling, and Hatch, Alden. *The Circus Kings: Our Ringling Family Story.* Doubleday, 1960.

Norwood, Edwin P. *The Circus Menagerie.* Doubleday, Doran, 1929.

*Otis, James. *Toby Tyler; or Ten Weeks with a Circus.* Harpers, 1909.

*Selby-Lowndes, Joan. *Circus Train.* Abelard-Schuman, 1957.

*Streatfeild, Noel. *Circus Shoes.* Random House, 1939.

Wallace, Irving. *The Fabulous Showman: The Life and Times of P. T. Barnum.* Knopf, 1959.

Zora, Lucia, and Cooper, Courtney Ryley. *Sawdust and Solitude.* Little, Brown, 1928.

Index

Bold face indicates pages on which maps or illustrations appear